Second Edition

READY TO WRITE

A FIRST COMPOSITION TEXT

KAREN BLANCHARD
Beaver College

CHRISTINE ROOT
Harvard University

Longman

A Pearson Education Company

This book is dedicated to the memory of Karen's father, Dr. Herbert Lourie, whose love of learning was an inspiration to all who knew him; and to the memory of Christine's mother, Charlotte S. Baker, who understood so well the power and magic of the written word.

Ready to Write: A First Composition Text, Second Edition

Credits appear on page 108.

Editorial Director: Joanne Dresner
Acquisitions Editor: Allen Ascher
Production Editor: Lisa Hutchins
Text Design: A Good Thing
Cover Design: Joseph DePinho
Text Art: Sue Smolinski
Production Supervisor: Anne Armeny

Library of Congress Cataloging-in-Publication Data
Blanchard, Karen Lourie
    Ready to write: a first composition text / by Karen Lourie
Blanchard and Christine Baker Root.—2nd ed.
       p.   cm.
    ISBN 0-201-85999-8
    1. English language—Textbooks for foreign speakers.   2. English
language—Composition and exercises.   I. Root, Christine Baker,
1945– . II. Title.
PE1128.B587   1994
428.2'4—dc20   93-21021
                                                          CIP

15 VG 01

Contents

Introduction

Ready to Write came about because of our threefold conviction that:

- lower-level students learn to write well and achieve a more complete English proficiency by learning and practicing composition skills simultaneously with other skills that they are learning;

- lower-level students are interested in and capable of writing expressively in English, however simple the language, on a variety of provocative and sophisticated topics if they are supplied with the basic vocabulary and organizational tools;

- ESL students need to be explicitly taught that different languages organize information differently, and they need to be shown how to organize information correctly in English.

Approach

Based on these assumptions, *Ready to Write* is intended to get students writing early in their second language acquisition experience. By providing them with a wide variety of stimulating topics to write on and exercises that go beyond sentence manipulation drills, students are encouraged to bring their own ideas and talent to the writing process. With a focus on paragraph development, students learn, step by step, the organizational principles that will help them express themselves effectively in English and the application of these principles to a variety of rhetorical formats.

As in *Get Ready to Write* and *Ready to Write More,* the activities are designed to encourage students to think independently as well as to provide them with many opportunities to share ideas with their classmates, thus creating a more dynamic learning environment. To this end, collaborative writing and peer feedback activities are included in all the chapters. In addition, great care has been taken to maintain an appropriate level of vocabulary and complexity of sentence structure for high-beginning and low-intermediate students so that the explanations, directions, and readings are easily accessible.

The Second Edition

This second edition of *Ready to Write* emphasizes the stages of the writing process by providing:

- **pre-writing** activities to help students get ready to write
- an abundance of opportunities for paragraph **writing**
- guidance in **revising** their writing
- activities for **editing** and **proofreading** their writing.

Two features from the first edition, "You Be the Editor" and "On Your Own," have been expanded to appear regularly throughout the text. "You Be the Editor" provides effective practice in error correction and proofreading in order to help students learn to monitor their own errors; an Answer Key has been provided for this section. "On Your Own" provides students with further individual practice in the paragraph-writing skills they have learned.

We hope that you enjoy working through these activities with your students. At any stage, they are definitely *ready to write.*

Organization: The Key to Good Writing

Organization is the key to good writing. Different languages organize their ideas differently. In English, organization means dividing your ideas into groups and putting them in a logical order. Before you begin to write and while you are writing, you will need to organize your ideas.

Organizing by Grouping

Look at the following list of places:

> South America
> New York City
> Italy
> Korea
> Istanbul
> Asia
> Tokyo
> Mexico
> Europe

This list can be organized by dividing it into three groups.

A	B	C
South America	Italy	New York City
Asia	Korea	Istanbul
Europe	Mexico	Tokyo

1. What do all the places in group *A* have in common?

   They are continents.

2. What do all the places in group *B* have in common?

   _____

3. What do all the places in group *C* have in common?

   _____

Each group can be further organized by giving it a name.

A	B	C
CONTINENTS	COUNTRIES	CITIES
South America	Italy	New York City
Asia	Korea	Istanbul
Europe	Mexico	Tokyo

By Schulz

© 1955 United Feature Syndicate, Inc.

Organizing Lists

Organize each of the following lists by dividing it into three groups. Remember to put similar ideas together and to give each group a name.

1. Sunday   winter
    January   spring
    February   Friday
    summer   December
    Tuesday

A	B	C
Name: *days*	Name: _____	Name: _____
Sunday	_____	_____
Tuesday	_____	_____
Friday	_____	_____

2. jet   truck
    bus   helicopter
    boat   submarine
    car   ship
    airplane

A	B	C
Name: _____	Name: _____	Name: _____
_____	_____	_____
_____	_____	_____
_____	_____	_____

3. Spanish   chemistry
    calculus   Arabic
    biology   geometry
    algebra   physics
    Japanese

A	B	C
Name: _____	Name: _____	Name: _____
_____	_____	_____
_____	_____	_____
_____	_____	_____

Often there is more than one way to organize things. Study the following list:

wine
roast beef
milk
potatoes
pork
carrots
beer
chicken
whiskey
spinach
juice
coffee

1.   First divide the list into *two* groups and give each group a name.

A	**B**
Name: _____	Name: _____
_____	_____
_____	_____
_____	_____
_____	_____
_____	_____
_____	_____

2.   Now divide each group again. Give each new group a name.

A	**B**	**C**	**D**
Name: _____	Name: _____	Name: _____	Name: _____
_____	_____	_____	_____
_____	_____	_____	_____
_____	_____	_____	_____
_____	_____	_____	_____

Can you think of something else to add to each group?

Making and Organizing Your Own Lists

1.   Make and organize a list of things you have to do this weekend.

2.   Make a list of all the people in your class. Organize the list by dividing the people into groups. There are many ways to do this. For example, you can have one list for females and another for males. How many ways can you think of to organize your classmates? Remember that all members of a group should have something in common.

3.   Make a list of all the things you *should* do when you are learning a new language. Make another list of all the things you *shouldn't* do.

Topics

When you made these lists, you put similar things together. You also gave each group a name. The name represented the main idea. We call the main idea the *topic*.

Choosing a Topic

Each of the following lists contains one word that is more general than the others. This word can be considered the topic of the list. Circle that word:

EXAMPLE: Spanish
           Japanese
           Arabic
           (language)
           English

A	B	C
Volkswagen	tennis	Washington
cars	soccer	Lincoln
Volvo	sports	Nixon
Mercedes	baseball	Carter
Ford	football	presidents

D	E
occupations	flowers
dentist	trees
teacher	vegetation
lawyer	plants
doctor	grass

Irrelevancies

When you are organizing your information, it is important to be able to recognize when something does not belong. When something does not belong, it is called *irrelevant*.

Identifying Irrelevancies

1. Each of the following groups contains one figure that is irrelevant. Find it and cross it out.

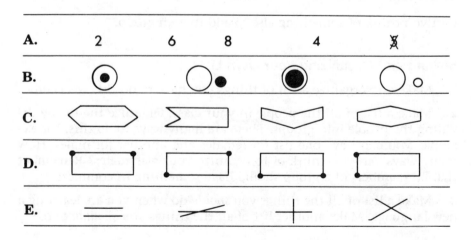

2. Cross out the word in each of the following groups that does not belong. Then write a topic for each list on the line provided.

EXAMPLE: _food_

candy
chicken
~~plants~~
vegetables

A. _____

green
dress
yellow
blue

B. _____

Pennsylvania
Philadelphia
Florida
California

C. _____

desk
chair
table
book

D. _____

Spanish
Turkish
Chinese
modern

E. _____

physics
swimming
biology
chemistry

F. _____

February
Wednesday
April
June

G. _____

king
president
prime minister
secretary

H. _____

tire
horn
steering wheel
Volkswagen

3. Read the following sentences and decide which ones are irrelevant to the topic. Draw a line through the irrelevant sentences.

EXAMPLE: Topic Sentence: It is interesting to visit foreign countries.

1.   You can meet new people.
2.   You can eat different kinds of food.
3.   ~~It is expensive.~~
4.   You can see the way other people live.

Number _3_ is irrelevant because _it does not support the idea that it is interesting to visit foreign countries._

a. Topic Sentence: There is a lot to do in New York City.

1.   There are many museums to see.
2.   It is the cultural center of the United States.
3.   The subways are dirty.
4.   The restaurants are interesting.

Number _____ is irrelevant because _____

_____

b. Topic Sentence: People prefer small cars for a number of reasons.

1.   They are cheaper to buy.
2.   They use less gas than bigger cars.
3.   They are easier to park.
4.   Some small cars do not have enough legroom.

Number _____ is irrelevant because _____

_____

c. Topic Sentence: Different people spend their free time in
different ways.

1. A lot of people spend their free time going to movies.
2. The price of movies has increased recently.
3. Some people like to read.
4. Many people enjoy sports.
5. Some people prefer to listen to music.

Number _____ is irrelevant because _____

_____

d. Topic Sentence: Smoking cigarettes is a bad habit.

1. It is expensive.
2. It may cause cancer.
3. There are many kinds of cigarettes.
4. The smoke often bothers other people.
5. Cigarettes left burning can cause fires.

Number _____ is irrelevant because _____

_____

Topic and Supporting Sentences

A paragraph is a group of sentences about the same topic. The main idea of the paragraph is usually given in the first sentence. This sentence is called the *topic sentence*. It introduces the topic and controls the information given in the other sentences. The other sentences add details to the topic and are called the *supporting sentences*.

Topic Sentences

Identifying Topic Sentences

EXAMPLE: The students in the class come from many different parts of the world. Some are from European countries such as France, Spain, and Italy. Others are from Middle Eastern countries, like Saudi Arabia and Israel. Many are from Asian countries like Japan. The largest number are from Latin American countries, such as Venezuela and Mexico.

What is the topic sentence?

The students in the class come from many different parts of the world.

Notice that all the sentences relate to the topic sentence.

Read the following paragraphs and answer the questions.

1.   There are many reasons why millions of Americans move every year. Some move to find better jobs or to advance their careers. Others are attracted to places with better weather. Still others want to move to a place with less crime. Finally, many people want to move to a place with a lower cost of living.

What is the topic sentence? _____

_____

Do all the supporting sentences relate to the topic sentence? _____

2.   Many men are now employed in what were traditionally women's jobs. For example, there are now twice as many male nurses as there were ten years ago. Since 1972, the number of male telephone operators has almost doubled and the number of male secretaries is up about 24 percent.

What is the topic sentence? _____

_____

Do all the supporting sentences relate to the topic sentence? _____

3. Throughout history garlic has had many uses. The Romans gave garlic to their slaves for strength and to their soldiers for courage. During the Middle Ages, some people used garlic to keep witches away. In the eighteenth century it was used to cure diseases. Even today some people believe that eating garlic can prevent colds.

What is the topic sentence? _____

_____

Do all the supporting sentences relate to the topic sentence? _____

4. Video games are very popular on college campuses in the United States. Most colleges have at least one video game. These games, which cost fifty cents to play, make hundreds of dollars per week and thousands of dollars per year! In many cases, the schools use the money from the machines for school improvements and scholarships.

What is the topic sentence? _____

_____

Do all the supporting sentences relate to the topic sentence? _____

Choosing a Topic Sentence

Choose the best topic sentence for each of the following paragraphs and write it on the line provided.

EXAMPLE:

a. The city needs the money.
b. The city needs money to fix the buses.
c. The state has lots of money.

The city needs money to fix the buses _____.

Many of the buses need repair work. City officials say there is not enough money to fix them. They will borrow money from the state.

1. a. Taxes should be raised.
   b. Many teachers are not paid.
   c. Tax money is used to build new roads.

_____.

The city needs more money and will have serious problems if it is not raised soon. We need money to pay for new roads and the repair of old roads. We also need money to pay teachers' salaries and to pay for services such as trash collection. In addition, more tax money is needed for financial aid to the poor.

2. a. Shopping is difficult.
   b. The stores are crowded at Christmas.
   c. It is better to do your Christmas shopping early.

_____.

It will be more difficult for you if you wait until just before Christmas. Many stores run out of the more popular items, so it will be harder for you to find what you want. The stores are also more crowded, and the lines are much longer.

3. a. Skiing is expensive.
   b. Skiing is a popular sport.
   c. Skiing has many disadvantages.

_____.

Many people enjoy it even though it is expensive and dangerous. A lot of people spend every winter weekend skiing, and many families go on winter ski vacations. Neither the high cost of equipment nor the severe cold keeps skiers away from the slopes.

4. a. Airplanes have changed our lives.
   b. Advances in technology have made the world seem smaller.
   c. The telephone was an important invention.

_____.

For example, a person can have breakfast in New York City, board an airplane, and have dinner in Paris. A businessman in London can instantly place an order with a factory in Hong Kong by picking up the telephone. Furthermore, a schoolboy in Tokyo can turn on a TV set and watch a baseball game being played in Los Angeles.

5. a. It is expensive to attend a university in the United States.
   b. There are many things to consider when choosing a university.
   c. A good education is important.

_____.

First of all, you must consider the quality of the university's academic program. The university's size and location should also be given careful thought. Finally, you must always be sure to consider the tuition before you decide which university to attend.

Writing a Topic Sentence

Decide what each of the following paragraphs is about. Then write a topic sentence in the space provided. Make sure your topic sentence is general enough.

EXAMPLE:

*Miami is a nice place to take a vacation*_____.

It is always sunny and warm. The beaches are gorgeous with soft, white sand and beautiful, blue water. There are many fine restaurants in the Miami area, and most of the big hotels offer terrific entertainment nightly.

1. _____.

He has collected stamps and coins ever since he was a child. He is very proud of his valuable collections. He also enjoys painting and drawing. Recently he has become interested in gardening. Out of all his hobbies, Paul's favorite one is reading. He tries to read at least one book every week.

2. _____.

First of all, the plumbing doesn't work properly and the landlord refuses to fix it. I also have noisy neighbors who keep me up every night. Furthermore, there are so many bugs in my apartment that I could start an insect collection.

3. _____ .

Some people hijack airplanes for political reasons. Others do it for financial reasons. Still others hijack airplanes because they want to be famous.

4. _____ .

To me, books are the most wonderful things in the world. I can pick up a book and be in another place or another time without leaving my room. I could spend my whole life reading books.

5. _____ .

I can't wait to come home from school to eat the delicious meals she has prepared. She is always experimenting with different ingredients and recipes. No one in the world can cook the way my mother does.

6. _____ .

It never starts in cold weather and uses too much gasoline. The horn and the left turn signal don't work properly. I wish I could get a new car.

7. _____ .

First of all, the work is very interesting. I learn new things every day, and I get to travel a lot. Secondly, my boss is very nice. He is always willing to help me when I have a problem. I have also made many new friends at my job. And last, but not least, the salary is fantastic.

8. _____ .

My plane was six hours late. The hotel was horrible. On the third day my wallet was stolen, so I lost all my credit cards. It rained every day I was gone except for one day, and on that day I got a terrible sunburn.

Compare your topic sentences with your classmates' by putting them on the chalkboard. Discuss the differences.

Remember that a topic sentence controls the information for the rest of the paragraph.

Supporting Sentences

Recognizing Irrelevant Sentences

The following paragraphs each contain one sentence that is irrelevant. Cross out that sentence and be prepared to explain why it does not belong in the paragraph.

1. Cats make wonderful house pets. They are very loving and friendly. They are also clean. They don't eat much, so they are not expensive. Many people are allergic to their hair. They look beautiful.

2. There are several reasons why many American women are waiting until they are thirty years old or older to have their first baby. Some women have good jobs and want to continue their careers. Many American couples have two children. Other women don't want the responsibility of having children until they are older. Still others are waiting until they are financially secure before they start a family.

3. Running has many positive effects on the body. First of all, it increases the efficiency of the heart and lungs. Running also helps the body develop greater physical endurance. However, many people

prefer swimming. Finally, it helps the body become more mechanically efficient.

4. The Japanese automobile industry uses robots in many phases of its production process. In fact, one large Japanese auto factory uses robots in all of its production stages. Some Japanese universities are developing medical robots to detect certain kinds of cancer. Another automobile factory in Japan uses robots to paint cars as they come off the assembly line. Furthermore, most Japanese factories use robots to weld the parts of the finished car together.

5. The packaging of many products is very wasteful. Often the packaging is twice as big as the product. Packaging is used to protect things that are breakable. Many food items, for example, have several layers of extra packaging. Most of these extra layers are absolutely useless.

Identifying Topic and Supporting Sentences

ACTIVITY 1

A. Read the following sentences about Springfield Academy, a boarding school for high-school students. There is too much information here for one paragraph. Some of the sentences are about the quality of education. Label these Q. Some are about the rules of the school. Label these R. With some of your classmates read and discuss all of the sentences.

1. _____ Springfield Academy is famous for the high quality of its education.

2. _____ Students are not allowed to leave campus without permission.

3. _____ Students are required to wear uniforms.

4. _____ The laboratories have the latest equipment.

5. _____ Stereos and televisions cannot be played after 7 P.M.

6. _____ Most of its graduates attend very good universities.

7. _____ Many of the students at Springfield Academy feel that the rules are too strict and old-fashioned.

8. _____ Students who do not maintain a B average are put on probation.

9. _____ Teachers assign a minimum of one hour of homework per class.

B. Now divide the sentences into two groups.

A Quality of Education	B Rules of the School
_____	_____
_____	_____
_____	_____
_____	_____
_____	_____

One sentence in each group is general enough to be a topic sentence. Find that sentence in each group and circle it.

C. Write these two groups of sentences in paragraph form in the spaces provided below. Put the topic sentence first.

Group A _____

_____

_____

_____

_____

_____

Group B _____

_____

_____

_____

_____

_____

ACTIVITY 2

A. Read the following sentences about San Francisco. Two of the sentences are topic sentences, and the rest are supporting sentences. Put a *T* in front of each topic sentence, and an *S* in front of each supporting sentence.

1. _____ San Francisco is usually warm and pleasant during the day.

2. _____ Some of the country's most famous restaurants and hotels are in San Francisco.

3. _____ There are many things to see and do in San Francisco.

4. _____ The city has many interesting tourist attractions.

5. _____ There are many excellent art galleries.

6. _____ The weather in San Francisco is very pleasant.

7. _____ It is never too hot or too cold.

8. _____ The nightlife is exciting.

9. _____ San Francisco has a ballet company, an opera house, and a symphony orchestra.

10. _____ It is cool and breezy at night.

11. _____ The winters are mild and it rarely snows.

B. Write the two topic sentences on the lines provided. Then list the relevant supporting sentences under the topic sentences.

A	**B**
Topic Sentence:	Topic Sentence:
_____	_____
Supporting Sentences:	Supporting Sentences:
_____	_____
_____	_____
_____	_____
_____	_____
_____	_____
_____	_____

C. Check your work with your teacher, and then write the sentences from group *A* in paragraph form. Notice that the first sentence is indented.

_____

_____

_____

_____

_____

_____

_____

_____

D. Now do the same with the sentences from Group *B*.

_____

_____

_____

_____

_____

_____

_____

_____

Writing a Paragraph

CLASS ACTIVITY: BRAINSTORMING

Work through the following steps in class:

1. Your teacher will put a topic sentence on the chalkboard such as:

      It is difficult to learn a new language.

2. What ideas can you and your classmates think of to support this topic sentence? As you think of ideas your teacher will write them in list form on the chalkboard. (Remember these are just ideas, so they don't have to be complete sentences or in correct order.) Copy the list from the chalkboard here.

_____

_____

_____

_____

3. After you have a complete list of supporting ideas, discuss them. Decide which should be included in the paragraph (which are relevant). Cross out the ones that are not relevant.

4. With your classmates and teacher, write the relevant ideas from the list in sentence form. Copy the sentences below.

_____

_____

_____

_____

5. Finally, write the sentences in paragraph form. Your teacher will write them on the chalkboard. Copy the finished paragraph below.

_____

_____

_____

_____

_____

Ready to Write

INDIVIDUAL ACTIVITY

1. Choose one of the following topic sentences and write a list of supporting details.

• Exercise is important for good health.

• Living in a foreign country is expensive.

• It is important for parents to teach their children about _____.

• _____ is a great place to visit.

Topic sentence: _____.

Details: a. _____

b. _____

c. _____

d. _____

e. _____

2. Several students should put their lists on the chalkboard. The ideas in the different lists will probably be very different even if the topic sentence is the same. Discuss and compare the lists on the chalkboard and decide whether all the things on each list are relevant.

3. Write your list in complete sentences.

a. _____ .

b. _____ .

c. _____ .

d. _____ .

e. _____ .

4. Write a paragraph based on your list.

On Your Own

Decide which of the following topics you want to write about:

- beaches
- babies
- soccer
- cars
- classical music
- your pet

1. Write five different topic sentences on your topic.
2. Choose the topic sentence that best fits the ideas you want to express in your paragraph.
3. List the details of your paragraph.
4. Organize the details of your paragraph.
5. Read your list and cross out any irrelevancies.
6. Write your list in complete sentences.
7. Write the topic and supporting sentences in paragraph form.

Organizing Ideas by Time and Space

Organizing Ideas by Time

Look at the four pictures. They tell a story, but they are not in the right order. Number the pictures so they tell the story in a logical time order. Then write one or two sentences describing what happens in each picture. Make sure your sentences are in the correct time order.

Picture 1: *A man and his dog found a nice place to sit on the beach.*

Picture 2: _____

_____

Picture 3: _____

_____

Picture 4: _____

_____

What clues helped you decide how to number the pictures?

When you organized the pictures, you had to think about the time order in which events happened. Similarly, when you write a paragraph, you will often find it necessary to order events according to the time they happened.

Using Time Order

1. The sentences below all belong to the same paragraph, but they are not in the correct order. Number them so that they follow a logical time order. Put a *1* in front of the sentence you feel should be first, and so on.

_____ As the family became larger and larger, finding names became harder and harder.

_____ Susan and Tom Beck were very eager to start a family.

_____ At last, when the tenth child was born, they couldn't think of a name at all.

_____ When their first child was born they decided upon a name very easily.

Now write the sentences in paragraph form.

_____

_____

_____

_____

_____

_____

Follow the same procedure with the following exercises.

2. _____ From his home in Mexico, he flew to New York City.

_____ From there he went to Europe and then to the Far East.

_____ José took a trip around the world.

_____ After traveling through the Far East, he went to South America and finally back home to Mexico.

_____

_____

_____

_____

_____

_____

3. _____ Even more of the resolutions were broken as the year went on.

_____ On January 1, Tim made ten New Year's resolutions.

_____ When the year ended, he realized that he had not kept a single resolution.

_____ By the time the month was over, he had broken half of the resolutions.

_____

_____

_____

_____

_____

_____

Using Signal Words

In order to show time relationships, you will need to use signal words to help guide your reader from one idea to the next. Study these sentences. The signal words are underlined. Also note the underlined punctuation.

> Jane had a busy morning.
> First, she cleaned the kitchen.
> Second, she did her laundry.
> Third, she cleaned the bathroom.
> Finally, she sat down to rest.

Fill in the blanks with the appropriate signal words.

> Poor me! I've had a terrible day. Everything went wrong. _First_____, my alarm clock didn't go off, so I woke up an hour late. _____, I was in such a hurry that I burned my hand when I was making breakfast. I got dressed so quickly that I forgot to wear socks. _____, I ran out of the house trying to catch the 9:30 bus, but of course I missed it. I was very upset because my boss gets angry if anyone is late for work. I decided to take a taxi, but then I realized that I didn't have enough money. _____, I walked the three miles to my office only to discover that it was Sunday!

Here are some more sentences with other signal words.

> Before Jane had lunch, she swept all the floors, and then she
> waxed them.
> Next, she cleaned her closets.
> Later, she worked in her garden.

Using Prepositions

It is important to use the correct prepositions to show time order relationships.

DATES: in February/in April/in July
        on Monday/on Wednesday/on Friday
        on June 30, 1951/on the 30th of June
        at the end of the year/at the beginning of August
        from 1998 to 2010

TIMES: at 5:00/at 7:30/at 9:45
        at night
        in the morning; in the afternoon; in the evening
        from 4:00 to 4:30

Fill in the blanks with the appropriate prepositions.

1. I lived in Detroit _from_ 1960 _____ 1968.

2. We lived _____ 141 Cater Street _____ Concord, Massachusetts.

3. Lynn was born _____ 1952.

4. She was born _____ October 31 _____ 4:00 _____ the afternoon.

5. I'll meet you for lunch _____ Tuesday _____ noon.

6. Ruth goes to London every weekend to visit her parents. She takes the train _____ Saturday _____ 9:00 _____ the morning and arrives in London _____ 9:30.

Writing Paragraphs Using Time Order

1. Look at the following schedule for Dr. Harry Alden, the director of the Center for English Language Programs at the University of Pennsylvania. He had a very busy schedule yesterday.

Write a paragraph about his day. Be sure to use signal words. Remember to begin with a topic sentence and to indent it.

Ready to Write

Monday April **9**

9-11: read applicants' résumés
11-12: meeting with the dean
12-1: lunch with Dr. Davis
1-2: interview applicants
2-3: observe classes

Now do the same with the following:

2. Margaret read a gardening catalog and decided that she wanted to plant a vegetable garden. She has to do many things before she can enjoy the harvest. Read the list and put the items in a logical order.

_____ Plant the seeds.

_____ Pick the vegetables from the garden.

___1___ Order the seeds from the catalog.

_____ Prepare the soil.

_____ Keep the garden free of weeds.

Now write a paragraph. Use the list as a guide. Remember the first sentence should be a topic sentence.

_____

_____

_____

_____

_____

_____

3. Vicki is having some friends over for dinner this evening. She has no food in the house, and she has no cash, either. Here is a list of things that she has to do, but they are not in the right order. Number them so they are in a logical order.

_____ Buy food for dinner.

_____ Go to the bank.

_____ Make dinner.

_____ Return home.

_____ Clean the house.

_____ Go to the grocery store.

Using this list as a guide, write a paragraph. Remember to use signal words.

_____

_____

_____

_____

Read the paragraph you have just written. Can you combine any of your sentences? Can you think of any other things Vicki might have to do before her friends arrive? Rewrite the paragraph, adding your new ideas.

_____

_____

_____

_____

4. The following time line gives you information about Babe Ruth, the famous American baseball player. Use this information to write a paragraph about his life.

February 6, 1895:   born in Baltimore, Maryland
          1914:   joined the Boston Red Sox
          1920:   sold to the New York Yankees
          1921–34: led the Yankees to seven pennants
          1936:   elected to the Baseball Hall of Fame

_____

_____

_____

_____

_____

_____

_____

5. Now do the same with this time line about the life of Elizabeth Blackwell, the first woman doctor in the United States.

February 3, 1821: born in Bristol, England

          1832: emigrated to New York City

          1849: graduated from Geneva Medical School in Geneva, New York

          1853: opened the New York Infirmary because, as a woman, she could not get a job in a hospital

          1868: opened the Women's Medical College of the New York Infirmary

          1875: assisted in founding the London School of Medicine for Women

          1910: died in Hastings, England

_____

_____

_____

_____

_____

_____

6. Choose a famous person who interests you. Find information about his or her life. Make a time line based on the information, and write a paragraph.

_____

_____

_____

_____

_____

_____

Organizing Ideas
by Space

1. Sometimes you will need to organize details according to where they are located in space. Study this floor plan. Then read the description that follows. Note the underlined prepositions and prepositional phrases.

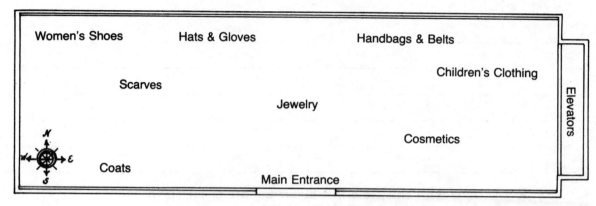

Lourie's is a large department store that sells clothing for the whole family. As you enter the store through the main entrance, the jewelry department is directly <u>in front of</u> you, <u>in the middle of</u> the store. <u>On your left</u> is the coat department, and the scarf department is <u>behind</u> the coats. <u>To the right of</u> the jewelry department is the cosmetics department. The elevators are <u>on</u> the east wall. <u>In</u> the northwest corner, you will find the women's shoe department. <u>Next to it</u>, <u>on</u> the north wall, are hats and gloves. <u>To the right of</u> the hat and glove department are the handbags and belts. The children's clothes are <u>between</u> the handbag and belt department and the elevators.

2. Here is the floorplan of the second floor of Lourie's. Fill in the floorplan below using the list provided.

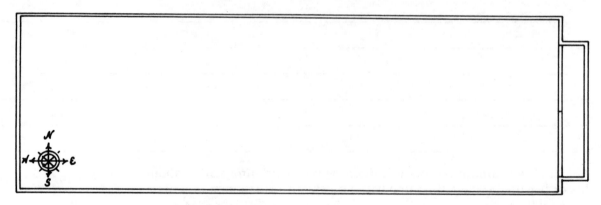

a. The elevators are on the east wall.
b. There is a large ladies' clothing department in front of the elevators. It covers the whole width of the store.
c. The men's clothing department is in the middle of the north wall.
d. To the left of the men's clothing department is the men's shoe department.
e. The college shop is in the southwest corner.
f. The junior shop is between the college shop and the ladies' clothing department on the south wall.

The location of the departments on the first and second floors of Lourie's is given in *space order*. There are two ways to organize a paragraph using space order. One way to organize by space order is to choose a starting point and give the locations of things in relation to that place. Another way to organize by space order is to describe the things in one area first, and then move on to the next area, and so forth.

3. Look at the picture and fill in the blanks in the sentences below with the correct preposition.

a. The customers are standing _____ the counter.

b. The jewelry is _____ the case.

c. The little girl is standing _____ her parents.

d. The saleswoman is _____ the counter.

e. There is a mirror _____ the counter.

f. The necklace rack is _____ the saleswoman.

4. The sentences in Exercise 3 above are not in the correct space order. Reorder the items below by numbering them from 1 to 6. Use the saleswoman as your starting point.

a. _____ The customers

b. _____ The jewelry

c. _____ The little girl

d. ___*1*___ The saleswoman

e. _____ The necklace rack

f. _____ The mirror

5. Now rewrite the sentences in Exercise 3 in correct space order.

_____

_____

_____

_____

_____

_____

Writing A Paragraph Organized by Space

ACTIVITY 1

This is a floor plan of the third floor of Lourie's.

Kitchen Equipment	Carpets	Lamps
Bath Shop	Furniture	
Electrical Appliances		Toys

Elevators

Write a paragraph describing the third floor. Use space order.

_____

_____

_____

_____

_____

_____

_____

_____

_____

_____

_____

_____

_____

ACTIVITY 2

Think about a recent storm that hit your area. As a class, write a paragraph about the storm. Your teacher will give you a topic sentence. For example: Last week we had a big snowstorm.

A. Each student should add one related sentence making sure that it contains at least one preposition.

B. When you have finished the paragraph, revise it so that the sentences make sense and are in a logical order.

On Your Own

Choose one of the following and write a description using as many prepositions as you can:

1. your typical weekday routine
2. your ideal weekend
3. the inside of your car
4. a beautiful flower garden

Organizing Ideas by Rank Order

Using Rank Order

One very common way to organize your ideas is to arrange them in order of their importance. You may begin with the most important idea and end with the least important idea, or you may begin with the least important idea and save the most important one for last.

Read this paragraph:

There are many ways to learn a new language. One way is to spend a lot of time watching TV and listening to the radio. Another way is to take classes at a language institute or university. But the best way to learn a new language is to talk to native speakers.

1. What three ways to learn a new language does the author mention?

_____

_____

_____

2. What does the author feel is the best way?

_____

3. Write the paragraph in another way. This time begin with the best way to learn a new language. Remember to begin your paragraph with a topic sentence.

_____

_____

_____

_____

_____

_____

_____

_____

_____

_____

_____

Signal Words

Study the following list of signal words for rank order. Notice that some of them are the same as those used with time order.

one (reason, way, advantage, method, etc.)	first
another (reason, etc.)	second
the next (reason, etc.)	third
the final (reason, etc.)	finally
the most important (reason, etc.)	most importantly
the best (reason, etc.)	for one thing
	first of all
	for another thing

Ranking in Order of Importance

Discuss the qualities of a good teacher with the people in your group. Decide which quality you think is the most important. Put a *1* in front of that quality. Then decide the next most important quality and put a *2* in front of it, and so on.

1. Qualities of a good teacher

    _____ has knowledge of subject

    _____ has ability to explain clearly

    _____ cares about students

Follow the same procedure with the following:

2. Things to consider when choosing a university

    _____ cost

    _____ location

    _____ quality of education

    _____ size

3. Advantages of marriage

    _____ having children

    _____ having companionship and someone to spend your life with

    _____ sharing money

    _____ sharing work

4. Difficult things about living in a foreign country

    _____ different language

    _____ unfamiliar customs

    _____ feeling homesick

5. Benefits of a higher education

    _____ have more employment opportunities

    _____ earn higher salary

    _____ gain prestige

6. Advantages of making your own clothes

    _____ lower cost

    _____ better fit

    _____ higher quality

Writing a Paragraph

ACTIVITY 1

Choose one of the topics in the preceding activity.

A. Write a paragraph based on this topic. Use the list provided for your supporting information. Begin with the one you feel is the most important. Remember to write a good topic sentence and use signal words.

_____

_____

_____

_____

_____

_____

_____

B. Now write the paragraph again. This time save the most important thing for last.

_____

_____

_____

_____

_____

_____

_____

_____

ACTIVITY 2

Choose one of the following topics to write about.

- Things to consider when choosing an apartment (or buying a house)
- Advantages of learning a foreign language
- Things to consider when recommending a restaurant
- Qualities of a good leader (or mother, doctor, politician, father, grandmother, babysitter)

A. Make a list of supporting ideas. Do not worry about the order.

_____   _____

_____   _____

_____   _____

B. Go over your list. Cross out any items that do not belong.

C. Now put your supporting ideas in order of their importance. Put a _1_ in front of the one you feel is the most important, and so on.

D. Write a paragraph about the topic you have chosen. Use your list as a guide. You may begin with what you feel is most important or save it for last.

_____

_____

_____

_____

_____

_____

_____

_____

_____

_____

E. Copy your paragraph on another piece of paper. Share your paragraph with your classmates.

Rewriting

Organizing your ideas and putting them in paragraph form are only the first two steps of the writing process. Next come the important steps of *revising* and *proofreading*.

Revising

It is almost impossible to write a perfect paragraph on your first try. The first try is called the first draft. You must *read over* your first draft carefully and answer the following questions.

1. Is there a topic sentence?
2. Do all the other sentences support the topic sentence?
3. Are the sentences in a logical order?
4. Did you include signal words to help guide the reader from one idea to the other?
5. Is there any other relevant information you want to add to your paragraph?

Proofreading

After you have revised your paragraph, you should rewrite it. Before you hand it in, make sure you proofread it. These questions will help you proofread.

1. Is the first sentence indented?
2. Are there any spelling or punctuation errors?
3. Are all the sentences complete sentences?

You Be the Editor

Read the following paragraph. It contains seven mistakes. Find the mistakes and correct them. Then rewrite the paragraph correctly.

Erik enjoy many types of sports. He is liking team sport such as basketball, soccer, and baseball. He also plays traditionals, individual sports like raquetball and golf his favorite sports involve danger as well as exciting. He loves parasailing, extreme skiing, and skydiving.

On Your Own

Choose one of the other suggested topics from this chapter, and complete the following steps:

1. Write the first draft of a paragraph on the topic you have chosen.
2. Revise the first draft. Use the revising checklist to help you. Copy the revised paragraph on a separate piece of paper.
3. Before you hand it in, proofread it.

Informing: Giving Information

CHAPTER 5

PEANUTS
By Schulz

© 1956 United Feature Syndicate, Inc.

Gathering Information

One way to gather information is by interviewing someone. In this activity, you will interview one of your classmates.

Before Writing
1. Make a list of questions that you want to ask your partner. Here are some suggestions.

a. Where are you from?
b. What is your native language?
c. Have you visited any other countries?
d. Do you know any other languages?
e. Are you married or single?
f. Do you have any children?
g. Why are you learning English?

You might also want to ask questions about your partner's

* family
* hobbies
* interests

* career or career plans
* education
* travel experiences

Copy your questions on a separate piece of paper. Leave enough space to write in your partner's answers.

Writing
2. You are writing an article about international students for your local newspaper. You want to include information about several foreign students. Write the paragraph of the article that describes the person you interviewed. Remember to begin with a good topic sentence and to group similar ideas together.

Revising
3. Now ask your partner to read your paragraph. Does he or she have any questions? Rewrite your paragraph based on your partner's suggestions. Remember to indent the first sentence.

Using Statistical Information

Sometimes you will want to use statistical information to support your topic.

Read the newspaper article. Notice that statistics support the main idea.

1. What is the topic sentence of this paragraph? _____

_____ .

2. What statistical information is used to support the topic sentence?

a. _____

b. _____

c. _____

Using Charts, Graphs, and Tables

Statistical information is often presented in the form of a chart, graph, or table. It is important that you be able to interpret the information and write about it. Here is some vocabulary that will help you:

increase	greater
decrease	rate
fall	percent
rise	percentage

ACTIVITY 1

Look at the pie charts. They show the strong trend toward urbanization in Mexico.

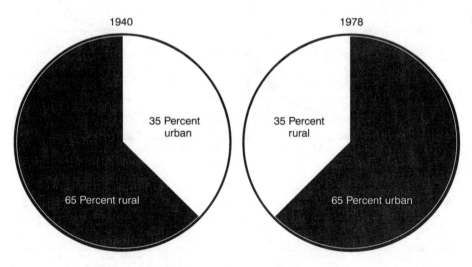

1940   1978

35 Percent urban   65 Percent rural

35 Percent rural   65 Percent urban

Answer the following questions:

A. What percentage of Mexicans lived in rural areas in 1940? _____

B. Did this percentage increase or decrease in 1978?

_____

C. What statement can you make about the percentage of Mexicans who lived in urban areas in 1978?

_____

D. Do you think the trend has changed between 1978 and now? Why?

_____

TEEN ROAD DEATHS CLIMBING EVERYWHERE

THE WORLD HEALTH ORGANI-ZATION, an agency of the United Nations, has just published the rather depressing results of a worldwide study on highway deaths. According to the 30-nation WHO study, there has been a dramatic increase in the number of deaths from auto accidents among people in the 15–24 year age group. The greatest increase was recorded in Mexico, where a 608% rise in the number of highway deaths was recorded. In the United States there was a 95% increase in the number of teen deaths resulting from auto accidents. The smallest increase was in West Germany, which had a 41% increase in road deaths.

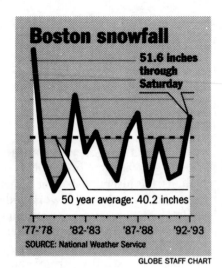

Boston snowfall

51.6 inches through Saturday

50 year average: 40.2 inches

'77-'78   '82-'83   '87-'88   '92-'93

SOURCE: National Weather Service

GLOBE STAFF CHART

ACTIVITY 2

Answer the following questions in complete sentences:

A. How much snow fell in Boston during the winter of 1992–93?

_____

B. How does that compare with the fifty-year average snowfall in Boston?

_____

C. What general statement can you make about Boston winters?

_____

D. If you were writing a paragraph about Boston's severe winters, what facts from the graph could you use to support your topic?

_____

ACTIVITY 3

The graph below shows the total number of students who attended Springfield Academy between the years 1985 and 1995.

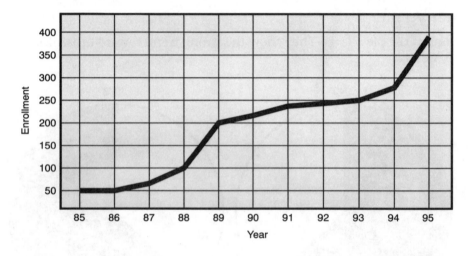

A. What general statement can you make about the number of students attending Springfield Academy between 1985 and 1995?

_____

B. In what year did the total enrollment double?

_____

C. When did the enrollment remain approximately the same?

_____

D. When was the greatest increase in enrollment?

_____

ACTIVITY 4

This graph is also about the enrollment at Springfield Academy, but it divides the total number of students into American and foreign students.

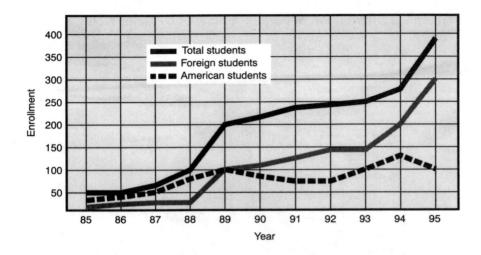

Answer these questions in complete sentences:

A. In what year was the number of foreign students equal to the number of American students?

_____

B. In 1988, how many foreign students attended Springfield Academy?

_____

C. In 1994, how many American students attended Springfield Academy?

_____

D. In what years did the number of American students remain the same?

_____

E. In what years did the number of foreign students remain the same?

_____

F. When did the number of foreign students increase the most?

_____

G. In what year were there twice as many foreign students as American students?

_____

ACTIVITY 5

Study the pie chart on page 34. What does it show? _____

_____

Percentage Distribution of Foreign Students by Major Fields

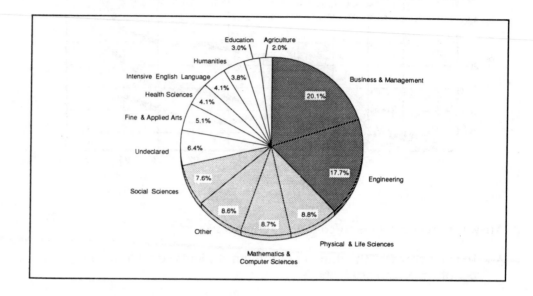

Answer the following questions in complete sentences:

A.   What generalization can you make about foreign students studying in the United States?

_____

B.   What is the most popular field? _____

C.   What percentage of all foreign students in the United States is studying engineering? _____

D.   What is the second most popular field? _____

E.   What percentage is studying business and management? _____

F.   This means that almost ____ percent of all foreign students are studying either engineering or business and management.

G.   This is followed by ____ percent studying social sciences and _____ percent studying physical and life sciences.

H.   What are some other fields that foreign students study?

_____

Writing: Paragraphs Using Statistical Information
ACTIVITY 1

You are in the process of setting up an English language program for foreign students. You have to write a report describing the program. Based on the information in the chart, you feel that the program should include a lot of instruction in technical English. Write the paragraph of the report that describes the percent distribution of foreign students by major fields. You may want to use rank order to organize your ideas.

ACTIVITY 2

A. Study this graph.

B. You are writing a letter to new members of your running club. Many of the new members are discouraged because it is taking them so long to run five miles. You want to explain the information in this chart. Answering the following questions should help you.

1. When does the greatest decrease occur? _____

2. How long does it take a typical runner to run five miles during the

   first year? _____

3. How long does it take during the second year? _____

4. What happens during the following five years? _____

5. How long does it take during the seventh year? _____

6. How many minutes does the amount of time decrease during the

   first seven-year period? _____

C. Using information from the graph, write the letter encouraging the members of your running club to keep running.

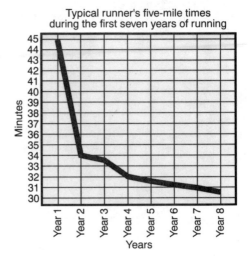

Typical runner's five-mile times during the first seven years of running

Combining Sentences

Sometimes you can make your writing more interesting by combining two short sentences with words like *and, but,* and *or.* Study these examples. Notice that a comma is placed before *and, but,* and *or.*

1. Combining sentences with *and.*

EXAMPLE:

She has a beautiful voice. She dances very well.
She has a beautiful voice, and she dances very well.

Use *and* when you want to add one idea to another.

2. Combining sentences with *but.*

EXAMPLE:

He worked all night. He didn't finish the project.
He worked all night, but he didn't finish the project.

Use *but* when you want to show contrast.

3. Combining sentences with *or.*

EXAMPLE:

You can study in the language lab. You can go to the library.
You can study in the language lab, or you can go to the library.

Use *or* when you want to give a choice.

Combine the following sentences. Use *and* to show addition, *but* to show contrast, *or* to show choice.

1. Jim is an excellent student. It's a pleasure to have him in class.

_____

_____

2. Diane didn't want to get up in the morning. She had to go to work.

    _____

    _____

3. Natalie wanted to go. Her mother wouldn't let her.

    _____

    _____

4. Do you think I should take English classes? Do you recommend French?

    _____

    _____

5. Donna was accepted at the University of Pennsylvania. She was accepted at Yale, too.

    _____

    _____

6. Micky and Bob will call when they get there. They'll send a telegram instead.

    _____

    _____

7. Ruth took her sister. Her brother was too young to go.

    _____

    _____

8. Natasha and Bill are going to have dinner. Then they are going to the theater.

    _____

    _____

9. The book was boring. Carmen read it anyway.

    _____

    _____

10. Kim has been in three movies. She has starred in several plays, too.

    _____

    _____

11. Yoko can sing very well. She can't play the piano.

    _____

    _____

You Be the Editor

Capitalization

Read this report about the history of the computer. All capital letters have been omitted. Correct the paragraph by putting capital letters in the proper places. You will need to add 18 capital letters. Remember these rules of capitalization:

1. Use a capital letter for names of people, countries, states, cities, towns, streets, days of the week, months of the year, and holidays.
2. Begin the first word of every sentence with a capital letter.
3. Begin the first word of a direct quote with a capital letter.
4. Capitalize the names of books, magazines, and movies.

> throughout history, people have found it necessary to do mathematical computations and keep accounts. in early times, we used groups of sticks or stones to help make calculations. then the abacus was developed in china. these simple methods represent the beginnings of data processing. as computational needs became more complicated, we developed more advanced technologies. one example is the first simple adding machine that mr. blaise pascal developed in 1642. another example is the first machine that would do calcualtions and print out results, which mr. charles babbage designed in 1830. in the middle of the twentieth century, researchers at the university of pennsylvania built the first electronic computer. today of course we have the computer to perform all kinds of advanced mathematical computations.

On Your Own

1. Make a graph of the results of the WHO study in the article on page 31. Write five sentences describing the data.

2. Look through newspapers and magazines for a chart or graph that interests you. Make a copy or cut it out of the newspaper or magazine. Write a paragraph explaining the data in the chart or graph.

3. With a partner, make up your own data for a chart or graph on a topic of interest to you. Then write a paragraph interpreting the data.

Expressing an Opinion

CHAPTER 6

By Schulz

© 1956 United Feature Syndicate, Inc.

Stating Your Opinion

When you write, it is often necessary to state your opinion about something you believe to be true.

ACTIVITY 1

Read the following sentences. Fill in the blank with the word or phrase in parentheses that you believe best completes the sentence.

EXAMPLE:

People are ___*too concerned*___ with the way they look.
(too concerned/not concerned enough)

1. It _____ all right for mothers with small children to work outside of the house. (is/is not)

2. Nuclear energy _____ necessary. (is/is not)

3. Women _____ be required to serve in the army. (should/should not)

4. Prayer _____ be allowed in the public schools. (should/should not)

5. It _____ justifiable to use animals for laboratory experiments (is/is not)

6. The U.S. government _____ spend more money on space programs. (should/should not)

7. People spend _____ money on their pets. (too much/not enough)

8. _____ is the most exciting sport. (Hockey/Soccer/Tennis)

9. Modern architecture _____ ugly. (is/is not)

10. UFO's (Unidentified Flying Objects) _____ exist. (do/do not)

ACTIVITY 2

The following useful phrases are often used to introduce opinions and generalizations:

> I believe (that)
> In my opinion,
> I think (that)
> I feel (that)

For each of the above sentences, write an opinion using an appropriate introductory phrase.

EXAMPLE: *In my opinion, people are too concerned with the way they look.*

1. _____ .
2. _____ .
3. _____ .
4. _____ .
5. _____ .
6. _____ .
7. _____ .
8. _____ .
9. _____ .
10. _____ .

What you have just written are simply your own opinions. They will be stronger with reasons, examples, or facts to support them. The following useful phrases are often used as signal words to introduce facts, reasons, and examples:

First of all,	Also,	For example,
For one thing,	In addition	Secondly,
One reason that	Moreover,	Thirdly,
		Finally,

ACTIVITY 3

Choose three of your opinions and give two or three reasons, examples, or facts to support them.

EXAMPLE:

Opinion *In my opinion, people are too concerned with the way they look.*

Reason 1 *They spend too much money on clothes.*

Reason 2 *They waste a lot of time looking at the way they look.*

Reason 3 _____

A. Opinion _____

Reason 1 _____

Reason 2 _____

Reason 3 _____

B. Opinion _____

Reason 1 _____

Reason 2 _____

Reason 3 _____

C. Opinion _____

Reason 1 _____

Reason 2 _____

Reason 3 _____

Writing a Paragraph

ACTIVITY 1

Choose one of your opinions and write a paragraph. Use your opinion as the topic sentence. Then use your reasons to write supporting sentences. Remember to use signal words.

The following questions will help you revise the first draft:

1. Is the first sentence indented?
2. What is the topic sentence?
3. Do all the supporting sentences support the topic sentence?
4. Are there any irrelevant sentences? Which ones? Why are they irrelevant?
5. What signal words were used to guide the reader?

ACTIVITY 2

Study the following list of sentences. They are all about children and TV. Some of them support the opinion that TV is good for children and some of them support the opinion that TV is bad for children.

1. TV exposes them to different countries, cultures, and ideas.
2. Children can learn about science, history, and the arts.
3. There is too much violence on TV.
4. Children see a false picture of human relationships.
5. Educational programs teach children basic skills such as reading and writing.
6. Watching TV is too passive. Children should be doing more creative and active things.
7. Children want to buy everything they see on commercials.
8. TV can be harmful to their eyes.
9. News programs inform them of what is going on in their community.
10. TV gives children free and interesting entertainment.

Before Writing

A. Divide the list into two groups.

TV is good for children	**TV is bad for children**
_____	_____
_____	_____
_____	_____
_____	_____
_____	_____

Writing

B. You are a concerned parent. The principal of your child's school has asked several parents to express their opinions about television for the parent-teacher newsletter. Which opinion do you agree with? Is TV good for children or is it bad? Use your opinion as the topic sentence for your paragraph. Use the reasons given as supporting sentences. Add any other reasons you can think of to support your opinion.

Revising

C. Read your paragraph again. Have you included signals to help the reader follow your thoughts? Now write your paragraph again, but this time include two of the following sentences. Be sure to choose the ones that support your opinion and put them in a logical place.

- There are over seven acts of violence per hour on prime-time TV.

- The most violent TV shows are on Saturday mornings, when many children are watching.

- When children see something on TV, they become interested and want to learn more about it.

- Children learn to recognize famous people.

- News programs teach children about important things that are going on in the world.

Read and Respond

ACTIVITY 1

Read the following letter and answer the questions that follow.

Dear Editor:

Last month our nine-year-old daughter was hit by a car. The man driving the car was drunk at the time and didn't stop at a stop sign. Our little girl was in the hospital for three long weeks. My husband and I didn't know if she would live or die. It was a terrible time for us. Although today she is alive, we are afraid something like that might happen again.

Recently we heard that the punishment for the driver was only a $200 fine. He didn't go to jail and he didn't lose his license. Today he is free to drive and possibly commit the same crime again. Maybe next time he will kill somebody.

We feel the traffic laws are not strict enough. Drunk drivers should pay for their crimes. We think their licenses should be taken away. We need stricter laws!

Yours truly,

Kathleen Johns

Kathleen Johns
Philadelphia, PA

Writing

A. Do you agree or disagree that we need stricter laws against drunk driving? Do you think people found driving after drinking should have their licenses taken away? Write a paragraph. State your opinion in the topic sentence.

Revising

B. Read your paragraph again. Do all your sentences support your opinion? Are all your reasons clear? After you have revised your paragraph, rewrite it. Can you include the following information?

–A U.S. Department of Transportation study found that drinking by drivers causes 25,000 deaths per year.

ACTIVITY 2

Read this news article and study the police report.

Computer Crime Hits Our City

Au
day
the
d in
the

ble.
opic
old
Eve
g to
ping
and
own
side
iere

but
ail's
tion
ard
f a
your
iese
ood,

NATIONAL CITY BANK and Trust Company is the largest bank in the city. Its assets are in the millions of dollars. In 1960 the bank computerized its operations. The bank considered itself very lucky because it had not been troubled by computer crime—until last week. On Wednesday, the accountants discovered that a total of $400,000 was missing from several different accounts. It is not yet known where the funds were transferred. Police investigation has led to three possible suspects. These three people had easy access to the computer system that transferred the funds out of the bank.

Police Report

(a) <u>Norman Glass</u>—Computer operator
 – has worked for bank six months
 – earns low salary
 – has wife and four children
 – lives in large house and drives expensive new car
 – before working at bank he served five years in Army
   (won a Medal of Honor)

(b) <u>Richard Allen</u>—Vice President of bank
 – has been with bank 35 years
 – good history with bank
 – recently lost a lot of money in stock market
 – takes expensive vacations
 – earns very high salary

(c) <u>Jim Tomlin</u>—Computer consultant
 – has worked for bank two years
 – is active in church and community
 – graduated top of his class at Harvard
 – supports widowed mother who is sick and lives in expensive nursing home
 – has a gambling problem

Before Writing

A. In small groups or with a partner discuss the situation and the three suspects. Together, decide who you think committed the crime.

Writing

B. Write a paragraph stating your opinion. Be sure to give specific reasons to support your opinion.

ACTIVITY 3

If you were the advice consultant for your newspaper, how would you respond to the following letters?

Dear Advisor:

My mother-in-law drives me crazy. She finds fault with everything I do. She thinks I don't take good enough care of her son. She criticizes my cooking and my housekeeping as well as the way I take care of our children. My husband says I should just ignore her, but that is difficult because she lives across the street. What do you think I should do?

Mrs. S. L.

A. Suppose you are the mother-in-law. Write a letter to *Dear Advisor* about your daughter-in-law. Write the letter from the mother-in-law's point of view. Share your letter with your classmates.

B. Now respond to this letter.

Dear Advisor:

My friend and I are having a terrible argument and we hope you can settle it for us. I say it's OK for girls to call boys on the telephone. I say it is all right for a girl to let a guy know she likes him and would like to go out with him. My friend disagrees. She says that men still prefer to do the courting, but women make it difficult now because they are so aggressive. She says men still prefer the old-fashioned type of girl. Who do you think is right?

Confused

C. 1. Share your responses with your classmates by either exchanging your papers or reading them out loud.

Revising

2. Revise and rewrite your response before you give it to your teacher. Look back to the revising checklist on page 28 to help you.

You Be the Editor

Read the following letter. It has eight errors. Find the errors and correct them. Then rewrite the corrected letter.

Dear Editor:

   In my opinion, it is important for women with small childrens to work outside of the home. First of all, is to difficult to be with little kids all day. Womens needs a break from there kids. Also, a woman who has a career can offer her children mores, because it is the quality of time that mothers spend with their children that are important.

Sincerely,
Lisa Harris

On Your Own

Write a paragraph giving your opinion on one or more of the following topics:

- Marrying someone of a different religion
- What society should do about crime
- Capital punishment

Describing Processes and Writing Instructions

Describing a Process

Whenever you need to explain the step-by-step order of how to make or do something, you are describing a process. When you write a process paragraph you will need to use time order to organize your ideas. You will also need to use signal words to help the reader understand the process.

Using Signal Words

Read the following paragraph. It tells how to make popcorn. The signal words have been left out. Write the appropriate signal words in the blanks. (Review signal words on page 39.)

It is very easy to make good popcorn. _____*First*_____, put three tablespoons of oil in a large heavy pot. _____, heat the oil on a high flame until one kernel of popcorn pops when you drop it into the hot oil. When the oil is hot enough, pour ¼ cup of popcorn into the pot and cover it with a lid. _____, reduce the flame to medium and begin to shake the pot gently. Continue shaking the pot until all the corn has popped. _____, empty the popcorn into a large bowl and add melted butter and salt.

Recognizing the Order of a Process

1. The sentences below describe the process of making a chocolate sundae, but they are not in the correct time order. Use the signal words to help you put the steps in the right order.

_____ Next, cover with whipped cream.

_*1*_ Chocolate sundaes are one of the easiest desserts to make.

_____ Finally, sprinkle chopped nuts on the whipped cream and top the whole thing off with a cherry.

_____ Then pour two tablespoons of hot fudge sauce over the ice cream.

_____ First, put one scoop of your favorite brand of ice cream in a dish.

Now write the ordered steps in paragraph form.

2. Put these steps in the right order.

_____ Then make a fist with one hand and grasp the fist with your other hand. Put your hands just below his rib cage.

_1_ The Heimlich maneuver is a method that anyone can use to help someone who is choking on a piece of food.

_____ Finally, press your fist into the victim's abdomen with a quick upward movement.

_____ The first thing you should do is stand behind the choking person and put your arms around his waist.

_____ If the person is still choking, you may need to repeat the maneuver.

Now write a paragraph.

3. Study the following series of pictures. They show the steps involved in repotting a plant. Then use the pictures to label the steps below in the correct time order.

_____ make a hole in center of soil

_____ press soil down with thumbs

_1_ cover bottom of pot with small stones

_____ drop plant into soil

_____ put two inches of soil on top of stones

_____ water plant

_____ add more soil until it almost reaches top of pot

Now write a process paragraph based on the pictures. The first two sentences are given here.

    When a plant grows too large for its original pot, it needs to be repotted. This can be done quickly and easily if you follow the right procedure....

Writing a Process Paragraph

Choose one of the following processes to write about.

How to: —plan a party

—make your favorite dish

—change a flat tire

—study for an exam

—make your bed

—plant a garden

Before Writing

1. Make a list of all the steps in the process. Be sure the steps are in the correct time order.

_____

_____

_____

_____

_____

_____

Writing

2. Write a paragraph describing the process. Use the list of steps as a guide. Be sure to write a topic sentence that clearly states the process that you are describing.

Revising

3. Now read your paragraph again. Can you think of any other steps or details that you want to add? Are all your sentences clear and to the point? Have you included signal words to help make the process easy to follow? Can you combine any of your sentences with *and, but, or*? Write your paragraph again.

Writing about a Scientific Procedure

Processes are very important in scientific and technical fields.

1. Study the following lab report.

WATER EXPANSION EXPERIMENT

Purpose: To show that water expands when frozen

Materials: A glass jar

Procedure:

1. Fill glass jar halfway with water
2. Mark the outside of the jar at water level
3. Put jar in freezer until water freezes
4. Observe new water level

Results: Level of frozen water is higher

Now read the paragraph below. It describes the process of the experiment.

A very simple experiment can be done to show that water expands when it is frozen. All you need is an empty glass jar. First, fill half the jar with water. Then mark the water level on the outside of the jar. After that, put the jar in a freezer until the water freezes. When the water is frozen, take the jar out of the freezer and observe the new water level. You will see that the level of the frozen water is higher. This proves that water expands when it is frozen.

a. Underline the topic sentence.

b. Circle the signal words.

2. You are a science student. Study this lab report.

SOLAR ENERGY EXPERIMENT

Purpose: To show that black is a better collector of solar energy than white

Materials: 2 tin cans
black and white paint
room thermometer

Procedure: 1. Paint cans—one black, one white
2. Fill cans with water
3. Put cans in direct sunlight for 3 hours
4. Check temperature of water in cans and compare

Results: Water in black can is hotter.

Using the information in the lab report, write a paragraph describing the process of the experiment.

Writing Instructions

1. Use the shapes and lines to make a simple drawing in the space provided in the box.

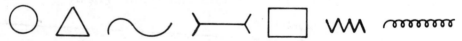

Writing
2. On a separate piece of paper, write instructions to one of your classmates. Your instructions should describe how to arrange the shapes so that your classmate's picture will look like yours. Be sure to write clear sentences and to put them in a logical order. This will help your reader to make an exact copy of your drawing.

3. Give your instructions to one of your classmates. Tell him or her to follow them in order to make a drawing like yours.

4. Compare your drawings. Are your drawings the same? If they are not, can you decide why? Was it because the instructions weren't clear enough? Can you improve your instructions?

Revising
5. Revise your instructions so that they are clearer and more precise. Then copy them onto a new sheet of paper.

Giving Directions

When you write directions, you are explaining the step-by-step order of how to get somewhere. The steps must be clear and in the correct sequence.

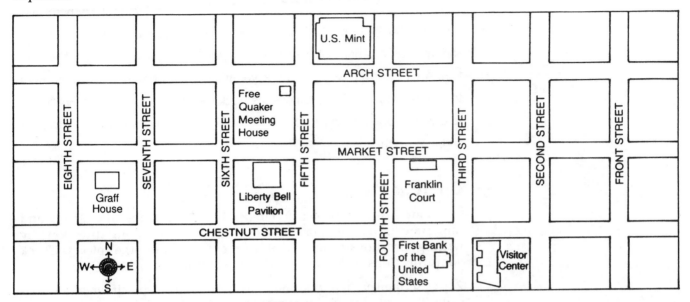

Look carefully at the map of the historical area of Philadelphia. Find the Visitor Center on the map. Where is it located?

_____

Read these directions:

In order to get from the Visitor Center to the U.S. Mint, follow these directions. First, go north two blocks from the Visitor Center. Then turn left on Arch Street. Continue two blocks on Arch Street to 5th Street.

What is located on the northeast corner of 5th and Arch Streets?

You work at the Visitor Center. Write directions from the Visitor Center to each of the following places for a tour guidebook.

1. Liberty Bell
2. First Bank of the United States
3. Free Quaker Meeting House
4. Franklin Court
5. Graff House

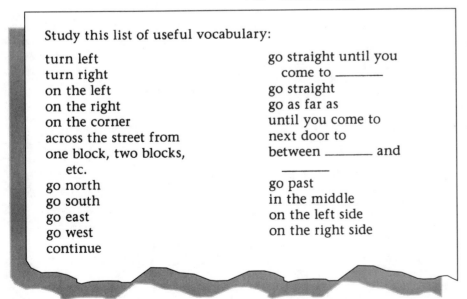

Study this list of useful vocabulary:

turn left	go straight until you
turn right	come to _____
on the left	go straight
on the right	go as far as
on the corner	until you come to
across the street from	next door to
one block, two blocks,	between _____ and
etc.	_____
go north	go past
go south	in the middle
go east	on the left side
go west	on the right side
continue	

You Be the Editor

Read the following paragraph. It has nine errors. Find the errors and correct them. Then, rewrite the corrected paragraph.

It is not difficult to remove the shell from a lobster if you follow these step. First, you should to put the lobster on it's back and remove the two large claws and tail section. After that, You must also twist off the flippers at end of tail section. After these are twisted off, use you fingers to push the lobster meat out of the tail in one piece. Next, remove the black vein. From the tail meat. Finally, before you sit down to enjoy your meal, break open the claws with a nutcracker and remove the meat.

On Your Own

1. Draw a simple map of your neighborhood. Label the streets and important buildings. Practice the vocabulary of giving directions by writing directions from several different places to other places. Check your directions by having another student follow them.

2. Describe the steps you must take to protect yourself when a hurricane, blizzard, tornado, or other natural disaster is forecast for your area.

3. Describe the process involved in getting or renewing your driver's license.

Writing Personal and Business Letters

Personal Letters

Letters to friends and relatives are informal letters. These letters do not have to be typed, and they usually follow the form below.

May 8, 1998 ⎤ date

Dear Daniel, ⎤ greeting

Thank you very much for the wonderful holiday vacation I spent with you and your family. Your mother is such a terrific cook! I think I must have gained 10 pounds in just the week I spent with you. I really appreciate your taking time off from work to take me around and show me so many places. You are lucky to live in such an interesting area. I hope that soon you will be able to visit my part of the country. Thank you again for a wonderful time. Let's keep in touch.

— message

closing — ⎡ *Best regards,*
signature — ⎣ *Matthew*

"It is important to state the purpose of your business letter immediately. Go directly to the point."

Remember these guidelines when you write a personal letter:

1. The date goes in the upper right corner. (The month is capitalized, and a comma goes between the day and the year.)
2. The greeting (Dear _____) is followed by a comma.
3. The closing (often "Love" in personal letters) is followed by a comma.

Use the following form for the envelope of a personal letter:

Matthew Graham
327 South 2nd Street
Philadelphia, Pa. 19106

Mr. Daniel Lowrie
52 Main Street
Cowby, Oregon 97013

Don't forget:

1. The return address of the person who writes the letter goes in the upper left corner.
2. The address (the address of the person who will receive the letter) goes in the center of the envelope.
3. The stamp goes in the upper right corner.

Ready to Write

Practice Writing Personal Letters

Write a letter to one of the following on a separate piece of paper. Bring your finished letter to class in a properly addressed envelope.

- A friend. Invite him or her to come visit you.
- Your aunt. Thank her for the gift she sent you.
- A friend you haven't seen recently. Tell him or her what is new in your life.
- Your parents. Tell them about an important decision you have made.

Business Letters

Business letters are formal letters. The form of a business letter is different from the form of a personal letter. Look at the sample business letter on the next page. Notice the differences between it and the personal letter on page 51.

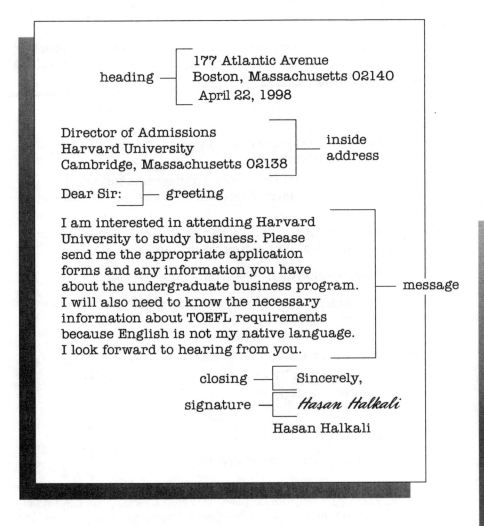

```
                    177 Atlantic Avenue
heading —           Boston, Massachusetts 02140
                    April 22, 1998


Director of Admissions
Harvard University                     inside
Cambridge, Massachusetts 02138         address

Dear Sir:  — greeting

I am interested in attending Harvard
University to study business. Please
send me the appropriate application
forms and any information you have
about the undergraduate business program.   — message
I will also need to know the necessary
information about TOEFL requirements
because English is not my native language.
I look forward to hearing from you.

              closing —   Sincerely,

            signature —   Hasan Halkali
                          Hasan Halkali
```

Remember these guidelines for writing business letters:

1. The greeting is followed by a colon.
2. It is important to state the purpose of your letter immediately. Go directly to the point. Be as brief and explicit as you can.
3. Type business letters if possible.
4. Do not ask personal information (age, health, family) of the person you are writing to.
5. Do not use contractions.

Practice Writing Business Letters

ACTIVITY 1

Read the advertisement for the Philadelphia Orchestra. Write a letter requesting tickets. Use the information below to help you. In your letter you will need to state:

1. whether you want a matinee or an evening performance.
2. the date of the performance you want to attend.
3. which price ticket you want.
4. whether you are including your credit card number or a personal check.

Make your letter short and to the point.

ACTIVITY 2

Do one of the following. Bring your finished letter to class in a properly addressed envelope. (Use the same format for a business letter envelope that you use for a personal letter envelope.)

- Write your own letter to a college admissions office asking for information.
- Write to a radio station requesting more information about a product you heard advertised.
- Write a letter stating that you ordered a magazine subscription three months ago and haven't received any copies of the magazine yet.
- Write a letter to a university informing the director of admissions that you have decided not to attend that university.

Answering these questions will help you.

1. Have you included both a heading and an inside address? Are they in the proper places?
2. Is there a colon after the greeting?
3. Is your letter direct and to the point?
4. Is the closing followed by a comma?
5. Did you sign your letter?

Use Your Imagination

Imagine yourself in the following situation:

Two weeks ago you called the person who lives above you in your apartment building. You were upset because he plays his stereo so loudly. He plays it very loudly all day long so it bothers you when you are trying to study. He also plays it late at night when you are trying to sleep. When you spoke with him on the phone, he said that he would try to keep the volume lower. The first few days it was better, but now it is becoming a problem again. Also, you are trying to study for your final exam. It is very difficult because of the constant noise.

1. Write a polite letter to him asking him to please be more considerate.

2. It is now one week later and the noise has gotten even worse. You are furious. Write an angry letter to your landlord threatening to break your lease and move out if he does not do something about the noise. Since this is a business letter, don't forget the heading and the inside address. Remember to type the final copy of a business letter.

Separating Formal from Informal Phrases

In each pair of sentences or phrases below, one should be used only in informal letters. The other phrase is appropriate for formal letters. Put an *F* in front of the one that is formal and an *I* in front of the one that is informal.

1. _____ I'm really sorry about what happened.

   _____ I would like to apologize for any inconvenience this may have caused you.

2. _____ I look forward to hearing from you soon.

   _____ I can't wait to hear from you.

3. _____ Dear Julie,

   _____ Dear Mrs. Brody:

4. _____ Yours truly,

   _____ Love,

5. _____ I will call you Monday morning.

   _____ I'll give you a call next week.

6. _____ I appreciate your help in this matter.

   _____ Thanks a lot for helping me.

You Be the Editor

Read the following memo from the president of Bayview Associates. The form is correct for a memo but there are eight mistakes. Correct the mistakes and rewrite the memo correctly.

MEMO

TO: All Employees
FROM: David Stanson, President
DATE: 3/13/98
RE: Punctuality

it has come recently to my attention that we are becoming increasingly lax about beginning our work day in 9 A.M. I understand that many of you are always on time and I thank you for your reliability, I also realize that sometimes lateness cannot be avoided. I feel, however, that habitual late has become a serious problem and that I must mention it before it gets worser. It is my opinion that we are a team and that we must all work together to build strongest company we can. Inattention to punctuality creates resentment among coworkers. I will appreciate it if you paying more attention to this important detail in the future.

Describing People, Things, and Places

The purpose of a description is to create a picture using words. The most important part of writing a description is using clear and effective words that create exactly the picture you want.

Describing People

Read this telephone conversation:

Lucia: I'm so glad you called me today. I have a big problem and I hope you can help me.

Clara: What's the problem? I'll help if I can.

Lucia: My cousin is coming home tonight from his trip to Europe and I'm supposed to pick him up at the airport at seven.

Clara: Oh? Is your car giving you trouble again?

Lucia: No. I just found out I have to work late tonight. Can you possibly pick him up for me?

Clara: Sure. What airline is he taking?

Lucia: Pan Am. Flight 607.

Clara: OK. But how will I recognize him?

Lucia: Well, he's medium height and average weight. He wears glasses, and he dresses very well.

Clara: That could be almost anyone. Can you be more specific?

Lucia: Well, his hair is blond and curly. I almost forgot! He has a beard.

Clara: What's his name?

Lucia: Ernie Norton.

Clara: OK, no problem. I'll find him.

Lucia: Thank you so much!

At the last minute, Clara was unable to go to the airport. Her brother agreed to pick Ernie up instead. Clara wrote him a note describing Ernie so that he would be able to find him. What did Clara's note say? The following questions should help you.

- Is he tall or short?
- Is he fat or thin?
- What color hair does he have?
- Is his hair curly or straight?
- Does he wear glasses?
- Is there anything about him that you notice immediately?

Write Clara's note to help her brother.

By Schulz

Ready to Write

Guess Who

Complete the following steps:

1. Choose someone in your class to describe.

Writing

2. Write a short description of that person, but do not mention his or her name. Remember to include details about height, weight, hair color, distinguishing marks, etc. Write your description on a separate piece of paper.

3. • Give the description to your teacher.

   • When the teacher has everyone's description, he will mix them up and give each student one of the descriptions.

   • Read the description you were given. Can you guess who it is?

Revising

4. Write your paragraph again so that it is clearer. Check the punctuation and capitalization.

Ready to Write

Write a Paragraph

Write a description of one of the boys in this picture. You might need to review the vocabulary with your teacher.

Describing An Object

You work in the advertising division of Lourie's Department Store. You are working on the holiday mail order catalog. You have just completed the first page.

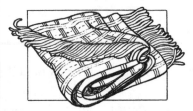

1. Keep warm this winter with this practical but good-looking plaid blanket. It is 52″ by 76″ and has fringe on two sides. It was handmade in England of the finest quality wool. $70. Stock number 922–5893.

2. Be on time with these accurate and elegant Swiss watches. Both the man's and the woman's have black leather bands and gold faces. The face of the man's watch is 1 ¼″ and the face of the woman's is ¾″. Both watches have a one-year guarantee. $180. Stock number 387–6359.

4. This beautiful, antique Chinese vase makes a perfect gift. It is 18″ tall and comes with a wooden stand. It has two handles and is available in blue or white. $200. Stock number 371–2311.

3. You'll love this soft cashmere sweater. It has long sleeves, a ruffled collar and five pearl buttons down the front. It comes in four colors: black, white, red, blue. It is available in sizes small, medium, and large. $85. Stock number 923–8363.

1.

Now write short descriptions of these pictures from the next page of the catalog. Use your imagination. Remember, when you describe an object, you will need to mention such things as shape, size, color, texture, and material.

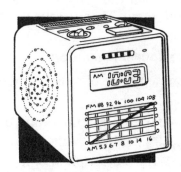

1. plaid, short-sleeved shirt with pocket

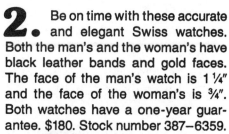

2. clock radio

3. leather pocketbook with one handle, zipper

Ready to Write

Guess What

ACTIVITY 1

A. Complete the following steps.

Before Writing
1. • Think of a familiar object to describe, such as a pencil, a chair, or a shoe.

   • Make a list of all the details you want to put in the description.

Remember to include details about size, shape, color, etc.

Writing
2. Write a description of your object, but do not mention what it is.

3. Read the description to your classmates and see if they can guess what you are describing.

ACTIVITY 2

In this activity, you will have to write a very clear description for your classmates.

Before Writing
A. Study the two pictures of chairs.

Make a list of descriptive details about each one.

_____   _____

_____   _____

_____   _____

Writing
B. Choose one chair and write a description of it. Try to be as clear as possible, but do not compare it to the other chair.

C. Exchange your paragraph with another group's paragraph.

Read the paragraph from the other group. Can you pick out which chair it is describing? Is it number *1* or number *2*?

What parts of the description helped you pick the right one? What parts of the description confused you? Write some comments on the paragraph and then give it back to the group that wrote it.

Revising
D. When you get your paragraph back, read the comments and think about them. Then rewrite your paragraph so it is as clear as possible.

Use Your Imagination

Draw a picture of a spaceship. Follow these steps:

Before Writing
1. Make a list of important details.

Writing
2. Write a description of it.

3. Give your description to a classmate and see if he or she can draw the spaceship from your description.

Ready to Write

Revising

4. Compare the two pictures (yours and your partner's). How are they alike? What are the differences? They should give you clues to help you revise your paragraph, making the details and description clearer. Revise your paragraph.

Describing a Place

When you describe a place, you want to tell your reader where things are located. In order to write this kind of description, you will usually use space order to organize the details. You may need to review the prepositions on page 22.

ACTIVITY 1

Choose one of the following places to write about.

- your favorite room in your house or apartment
- your favorite place to study
- your office or classroom

Now work through these steps:

Before Writing

A. Draw a diagram of the room. Make a list of the details you need in order to describe the room, such as furniture, windows, etc.

Writing

B. Write a paragraph describing the room. Use spatial order to organize your paragraph.

C. Proofread your paragraph. Have you used the correct prepositions of place? Are the details logically organized? Copy your description on another piece of paper.

D. Exchange your paper with a partner. Ask him or her to read your paragraph and to draw a diagram of the room you described.

E. Do the same thing with your partner's paragraph. Compare the diagram you drew of your partner's room with the original one. He or she should do the same. Are there any differences between the diagrams? If yes, discuss them with your partner. Can you think of any way to make your paragraphs clearer?

Revising

F. Rewrite your paragraph with the changes you and your partner discussed.

ACTIVITY 2

Read the following conversation:

Helen: It's so crowded in here. I don't see any empty tables, do you?

Bill: No. I hope we don't have to stand up while we eat our lunch.

Helen: The smoke is really starting to bother my eyes. Do you want to go someplace else to eat?

Bill: That's not a bad idea. The music is so loud that I can hardly hear you.

Helen: Oh! Look! Connie and Jim are here!

Bill: Where? I don't see them.

Helen: They're over in the corner, next to the juke box.

Bill: There are two empty chairs at their table. Let's go sit with them.

Where do you think Helen and Bill are having this conversation?

Use your imagination! Write a short description of the above place.

You Be the Editor

Read the following description of a man wanted by the police. It contains nine mistakes. Correct the mistakes and rewrite the paragraph.

The police is looking for a tall, teenaged boy with blues eyes in connection with a robbery yesterday at Dayton's Jewelry Store. According to an eye witness, the robbery is approximately six foots two inches tall, very thin, and his skin is a very light color. He has dark, straight hairs. He has a broad shoulders and a dimple in his chin. His most distinguishing mark is a mole behind his right eye. He was last seen wearing a brown suede jacket and a brown pant. If you see anyone fitting this description, contact the police department immediately.

On Your Own

A friend is considering moving to the city or town where you live. Write a letter describing the city or town. Advise him about where he should live if he moves, and give the advantages and disadvantages of the area.

Reporting

Reporting What Happened

Reporting what happened is like telling a story. You will usually use time order to organize your ideas.

An important function of newspapers is reporting what happened. Read the following newspaper article. It reports what happened to Rob and Laurie Roberts and their dog, Bo. A report usually tells *who, what, when, where* and *why*.

> "Reporting a personal experience can be an effective way of supporting an idea."

DOG HERO IS HONORED

This dog hero was only 9 months old when he performed his brave act. Bo, a Labrador Retriever, won the annual hero award from the Ken-L Ration dog food company. His prizes included a gold medal, a gold collar and leash, and a year's supply of dog food! He also won $1000 for his owners.

Bo's brave deed happened last June. Bo and his owners, Rob and Laurie Roberts, were going down the Colorado River rapids in a 16-foot boat. The Roberts family lives near the river in Glenwood Springs, Colorado. Both of the Roberts and Bo are goods swimmers. The Roberts also love boating. The June trip was Bo's first time in a boat.

Things were fine until, as Laurie Roberts said, "A six-foot wave broke in front of us and filled the boat with water. Another big wave caught us from the back and flipped the boat over." Rob was thrown clear, but Laurie and Bo were trapped under it. "Every time I tried to escape, my head hit the boat," Laurie said. "I hit the bottom of the river several times. I realized I was drowning."

Rob picks up the story. "I reached the shore and looked for Laurie," he said. " I saw Bo swim out from under the overturned boat. Then he turned around and dived. Soon he cam back up, pulling Laurie by the hair." Laurie, scared and breathless, tried

to grab Bo. But the dog stayed out of reach, as if knowing they would both drown if Laurie pulled him under. Finally Laurie grabbed Bo's tail. He dragged her 30 yards to shore. Laurie was cut and bleeding, but she wasn't badly hurt.

"If it hadn't been for Bo, I wouldn't be here," Laurie told the audience at the Dog Hero awards dinner.

Ken-L Ration has been giving Dog Hero awards for 29 years. In that time, hero dogs have been honored for saving the lives of 306 people.

The following sentences are based on the story reported in the newspaper article. They are not in the correct order. Put a number *1* in front of the event that happened first, and so on.

_____ Rob swam to shore and began looking for Laurie.

_____ Another big wave came from the back and caused the boat to turn over.

_____ Bo saved Laurie by dragging her safely to the shore.

_____ Rob, Laurie, and their dog, Bo, took a boat ride down the Colorado River rapids.

_____ A six-foot wave filled the boat with water.

_____ Rob escaped safely, but Laurie and Bo were trapped under the boat.

Writing a Paragraph

1. Read the news release.

Pretend you live in southeastern Florida. Write a personal letter to a friend telling about the storm and the effects it had on you, your family, and your town.

2. Write a paragraph reporting on one of the following. First, make a list of your ideas. Then put the ideas into proper time order. When you write the paragraph, be sure to include signal words of time order.

- A sporting event you have attended.
- A recent event in your school or community.
- An accident that you have witnessed.

Revising
Revise and rewrite your paragraph. Use the following checklist to help you.

a. Is there a clear topic sentence?
b. Are all of the ideas in the proper time order?
c. Have you included appropriate signal words?

Supporting Your Ideas by Reporting a Personal Experience

Reporting a personal experience can be an effective way of supporting an idea.

1. The following are well-known sayings.

- Don't count your chickens before they hatch.
- Money is the root of all evil.
- Two heads are better than one.
- Variety is the spice of life.
- Haste makes waste.

Choose one of these sayings and write a paragraph about it. Use an experience from your own life to prove or disprove the saying. Before you write, you may want to discuss the sayings in class.

Ready to Write

HURRICANE STRIKES — MANY HURT

August 3. Hurricane Louann hit Southeastern Florida today causing death and destruction everywhere. Many orange and grapefruit crops were completely ruined by the storm which had winds that blew up to 150 miles per hour. Many people lost their homes or offices because of high winds, heavy rains and very rough seas. The Red Cross estimates that the killer storm caused many injuries. Also, millions of dollars worth of farm animals were killed due to the storm. It will take the people of Florida a long time to recover from the effects of this hurricane.

Writing

2. Write a paragraph based on one of the following sentences. Use a personal experience to support the main idea.

- Good things happen when you least expect them.
- Sometimes hard work is not rewarded.
- Things often don't turn out the way you planned.

Revising

3. Write your paragraph again, checking for content, grammar, punctuation, and capitalization.

Reporting What Someone Said

Using Quotations

Often in your writing you will need to report exactly what someone said.

Julie said, "The train is five minutes late."

Mark asked, "When does the party start?"

Remember these rules:

1. Put the speaker's exact words inside quotation marks.
2. A comma separates the quotation from the rest of the sentence.
3. Capitalize the first word of the quote.
4. Put periods, commas, or question marks inside the final quotation mark.

ACTIVITY 1

Rewrite the following as quotations on the lines provided. Put capital letters, quotation marks, commas, periods, and question marks where they are necessary.

1. mr whitnall said the office opens at 9:00

_____

2. the saleswoman asked do you want to charge this

_____

3. the teacher said study the first two chapters

_____

4. dr matsumi said take these pills three times a day

_____

5. the nurse asked do you feel better today

_____

6. the foreign student asked where is the library

_____

7. betty asked how did you enjoy the play

_____

8. suzanne said i love to travel

_____

9. gerald said running is good for your health

_____

Sometimes you will want to quote someone who is an authority on a topic you are writing about. This can make your paragraph stronger. In this activity you will practice adding quotations to make a paragraph stronger.

ACTIVITY 2

Read the following paragraph.

> The rising cost of energy has had many effects on the daily lives of people all over the world. Most people are really trying to conserve gas and oil. As a result, there have been many changes in life style. For one thing, people are buying smaller, more fuel-efficient cars. They are also moving back into the cities so they won't have to drive so far to work. In addition, some people are taking fewer vacations because of the high cost of fuel. When they do go on vacation, they are often going to places closer to their home town. Finally, people are trying to use less heat in the winter and to use their air conditioners less frequently during the summer.

The following quotations can be used to support the ideas in the paragraph. Rewrite the paragraph, adding these quotes where they belong.

"Americans, for example, have decreased their energy consumption by 20 percent since 1975." (Professor Stephen L. Feldman, director, The Energy Center, University of Pennsylvania)

"Energy conservation has become a preoccupation." (Christopher Byron, *Time*, December 22, 1980, page 55)

ACTIVITY 3

Now do the same with the following.

> After twenty years of being very successful, fast-food restaurants are no longer doing as well as they were. At this point, the $10 billion dollar fast-food hamburger business is having trouble. There are three major reasons for this. The first reason is the increase in the cost of beef over the past three years. The second reason is that people are becoming tired of hamburgers. The third reason is called saturation. That means that there are too many fast-food restaurants.

"A diet of hamburgers, french fries, and milkshakes just no longer satisfies the fast-food consumer." (Jack Goodall, president of Jack-in-the-Box Restaurants)

"There may be too many fast-food restaurants chasing too few customers." (Jeff Blyskal—manager)

You Be the Editor

Read the following magazine article about dieting. It contains eight mistakes. Fix the mistakes and rewrite the article correctly.

Do Diets Work?

Doctors and dieters agree that is possible to lose weight by dieting. The difficulty part, they report, is keeping the weight of after you to lose it.

Research indicates that many people successfully lose weight at some point in life, but most people gain the weight back within three years. Ian Fenn is a doctor who specializes in weight problems. He says that there is many sorts of diets, and medical science is working to figure out how to control body weight. "It is also a matter", he says, "of getting people to change their lifestyles. Each person need to find the right combination of diet and exercise for them."

On Your Own

1. Read the following dialogs and fill in the missing parts. Notice that when you write this kind of dialog, you do not use quotation marks.

A. Ruth: My sister had a baby yesterday morning!

Eleanor: _____

Ruth: It was a girl.

Eleanor: _____

Ruth: Seven pounds.

B. Natalie: We went to a fabulous new restaurant last night called Colette's.

Jim: _____

Natalie: I can't remember the exact address, but it's downtown, near City Hall.

Jim: _____

Natalie: I had lobster for the main course.

Jim: _____

Natalie: Great! I had the chocolate pie.

This is a telephone conversation between Bob and Pam. Only Pam's part is written. Fill in Bob's part.

c.   Bob: _____

       Pam: Hi Bob! How are you?

       Bob: _____

       Pam: How was your exam?

       Bob: _____

       Pam: That's too bad.

       Bob: _____

       Pam: Friday night? I don't have any plans yet.

       Bob: _____

       Pam: Sure. I love dinner parties.

       Bob: _____

       Pam: See you at 7:30.

Now fill in Diane's part.

d.   Diane: _____

       Janie: This is Janie.

       Diane: _____

       Janie: Yes, I went to school today. Why didn't you go?

       Diane: _____

       Janie: I hope you feel better now.

       Diane: _____

       Janie: We finished almost all of Chapter 8.

       Diane: _____

       Janie: Don't worry. I'll go over it with you before the test.

       Diane: _____

       Janie: You're welcome. See you tomorrow!

2. Choose one of the dialogues above and write a paragraph about it on a separate sheet of paper. Include direct quotations in your paragraph. Don't forget to use proper punctuation and quotation marks.

Comparing and Contrasting

Very often in your writing you will need to show how things are similar or different. When you *compare* two things, you show how they are similar. When you *contrast* two things, you show how they are different.

Study these two pictures:

Discuss these pictures with your classmates. Make a list of the similarities and another list of the differences.

Similarities	Differences
_____	_____
_____	_____
_____	_____
_____	_____
_____	_____

The Language Of Comparison

ACTIVITY 1

Study the following patterns of comparison:

A. Affirmative sentences

(1) With BE
John is a student. George is a student.

  a. John is a student and George *is* too.
  b. John is a student and so *is* George.

(2) With OTHER VERBS
Japan exports cars. Germany exports cars.

  a. Japan exports cars and Germany *does* too.
  b. Japan exports cars and so *does* Germany.

B. Negative Sentences

(1) With BE
The blue dress isn't expensive. The green dress isn't expensive.

  a. The blue dress isn't expensive, and the green dress *isn't* either.
  b. The blue dress isn't expensive, and neither *is* the green dress.

(2) With OTHER VERBS
Owls don't sleep at night. Mice don't sleep at night.

  a. Owls don't sleep at night, and mice *don't* either.
  b. Owls don't sleep at night, and neither *do* mice.

Practice using these structures. Follow the example.

EXAMPLE: Alan runs four miles a day. Peter runs four miles a day.

a. *Alan runs four miles a day and Peter does too.*

b. *Alan runs four miles a day and so does Peter.*

1. Mark plays the piano. Dave plays the piano.

a. _____

b. _____

2. The bank opens at 9 A.M. The grocery store opens at 9 A.M.

a. _____

b. _____

3. Jamaica is sunny and beautiful. Hawaii is sunny and beautiful.

a. _____

b. _____

4. Peter doesn't smoke. Alex doesn't smoke.

a. _____

b. _____

5. Skiing is an exciting sport. Surfing is an exciting sport.

a. _____

b. _____

6. The Browns don't have a car. The Johnsons don't have a car.

a. _____

b. _____

7. Philadelphia is an old city. Boston is an old city.

a. _____

b. _____

8. Suzanne lives in a small apartment. Karen lives in a small apartment.

a. _____

b. _____

9. Charlie isn't friendly. Liz isn't friendly.

a. _____

b. _____

10. Children need love. Adults need love.

a. _____

b. _____

ACTIVITY 2

Now study these patterns of comparison

1. The same _____ as _____

Carla speaks the same language as José.
This book is the same price as that one.
My house is the same color as yours.

2. as _____ as _____

Sam is as tall as his father.
Pam is as serious as Anne.
Women's clothes are as expensive as men's clothes.
Dick drives as carefully as Mary.
Charlotte dresses as well as Stephanie.

Practice using these patterns. Follow the example.

EXAMPLE: Danny weighs 185 lbs. Arthur weighs 185 lbs.

(weight) _Danny is the same weight as Arthur._

(heavy) _Danny is as heavy as Arthur._

1. Mary is five feet tall. John is five feet tall.

(height) _____

(tall) _____

2. This car costs $8,500. That car costs $8,500.

(price) _____

(expensive) _____

3. My house has twelve rooms. Your house has twelve rooms.

(size) _____

(big) _____

4. Jeffrey was born in 1982. Paul was born in 1982.

(age) _____

(old) _____

5. This story is seventy pages long. That story is seventy pages long.

(length) _____

(long) _____

ACTIVITY 3

Study the following vocabulary which you will need to make comparisons:

similar to	both
similar	have...in common
and...too	the same as
and...either	as...as
and so...	be like
and neither...	

Write a sentence of comparison for each of the following pairs of words. Use a variety of structures and vocabulary.

EXAMPLE: The Empire State Building / the Statue of Liberty

The Empire State Building is in New York City and so is the Statue of Liberty.

1. England / United States

_____

2. Abraham Lincoln / John F. Kennedy

_____

3. lemons / bananas

_____

4. tennis / ping pong

_____

5. chemistry / biology

_____

Recognizing Similarities

Read the following paragraph.

The Reporter and *The Monitor* are very similar weekly magazines that report on the political, financial, and cultural events of the world. Both of these popular magazines cost $1.25, and both are read by millions of people around the world. They have the same cover story almost every week, and they usually review the same books and movies in their literature and cinema sections. Another similarity between the two magazines is their point of view. *The Reporter* is very conservative and so is *The Monitor*. Finally, both magazines are translated into many languages.

1. Underline all the expressions of comparison.

2. Make a list of the similarities between the two magazines.

_____   _____

_____   _____

_____   _____

_____   _____

_____   _____

Writing Comparative Sentences

ACTIVITY 1

These sentences are based on the paragraph above. Rewrite each sentence using the words in parentheses. You may need to refer back to the paragraph.

EXAMPLE: *The Monitor* and *The Reporter* are both weekly magazines.

(and so)   *The Monitor is a weekly magazine, and so is The Reporter.*

1. Both *The Monitor* and *The Reporter* are weekly magazines.

    (and so)   _____

2. *The Monitor* and *The Reporter* report on political, financial, and cultural events of the world.

    (and . . . too)   _____

3. Both magazines cost $1.25.

    (the same . . . as)   _____

4. *The Reporter* is very conservative and so is *The Monitor*.

    (both)   _____

5. Both magazines are translated into many languages.

    (as . . . as)   _____

ACTIVITY 2

Write five sentences comparing Julie Aronson and Emily Burr. Base your comparisons on the information provided on their driver's licenses.

1. _____
2. _____
3. _____
4. _____
5. _____

ACTIVITY 3

Study the following ads. Write five sentences of comparison based on your observations and the information provided.

Lourie's

Ladies' blouse

Machine washable
Permanent Press
Sizes 8–14
red, navy, white, green
$23

Green's

Ladies' blouse

Machine washable
Permanent Press
Sizes 8–14
red, navy, white, green
$23

1. _____
2. _____
3. _____
4. _____
5. _____

Writing a Paragraph of Comparison

ACTIVITY 1

A. Look at this biographical information about two important Americans, Benjamin Franklin and Thomas Jefferson.

**BENJAMIN FRANKLIN
1706–1790**

- Founded University of Pennsylvania
- Famous inventor
- Helped write the Declaration of Independence
- Important man in American Revolution
- Well-known philosopher and thinker
- Ambassador to France

**THOMAS JEFFERSON
1743–1826**

- Author of Declaration of Independence
- 3rd President of United States
- Foreign Minister to France
- Founded University of Virginia
- Philosopher, architect, inventor
- Important man in American Revolution

Before Writing
B. Make a list of the similarities between the two men.

_____   _____

_____   _____

_____   _____

_____   _____

Writing
C. Now, write a paragraph comparing these two famous men. Use your list of similarities as a guide.

ACTIVITY 2

A. Choose one of the following topics to write a comparison about.

- two movies you have seen
- two restaurants you have been to
- two teachers you have had
- two sports you enjoy
- two people you know

Before Writing
B. Before you begin to write the first draft of your paragraph, make a list of similarities between the two things you are comparing.

_____   _____

_____   _____

_____   _____

_____   _____

Writing
C. Use the list as your guide to write a paragraph of comparison.

The Language Of Contrast

Ann and Beth are identical twins. Of course, they are alike in many ways. They are the same age, the same height, and the same weight. They also have the same color eyes and hair. However, they are also different in many ways. Study the following patterns:

1. Ann is *funnier than* Beth.
   Ann is *busier than* Beth.
   Ann is *cuter than* Beth.
   Ann is *nicer than* Beth.
   Ann is *smarter than* Beth.

2. Beth is *more serious than* Ann.
   Beth is *more athletic than* Ann.
   Beth is *more creative* than Ann.
   Beth is *more interesting than* Ann.
   Beth is *more sophisticated than* Ann.

We use *-er* and *more* when we are contrasting two things.
What kind of words use *-er*?

_____

What kind of words use *more*?

_____

Now study these patterns. We use *-est* and *most* to contrast three or more things.

1. Janie is the *nicest* person in the class.
   Jim is the *tallest* man in the class.
   Cathy is the *busiest* person in the class.

2. This is the *most important* chapter in the book.
   This is the *most valuable* diamond in the store.
   This is the *most expensive* car in the parking lot.

What kind of words use *-est*?

_____

What kind of words use *most*?

_____

Notice these common exceptions:

good	better	the best
well	better	the best
bad	worse	the worst
badly	worse	the worst

ACTIVITY 1

Practice using these patterns. Follow the example.

EXAMPLE: Gary weighs 178 lbs. Gerald weighs 165 lbs.
Gary is heavier than Gerald.
_____

1. The Nile is 4,145 miles long. The Amazon is 3,915 miles long.

2. Mt. Everest is 29,025 feet high. Mt. Fuji is 12,389 feet high.

_____

3. The Pacific Ocean is 36,198 feet deep. The Atlantic Ocean is 28,374 feet deep.

_____

4. The third chapter is very difficult. The fourth chapter isn't as difficult.

_____

5. Ann is a very careful driver. Paul isn't a very careful driver.

_____

ACTIVITY 2

Study these expressions of contrast:

;however,	more than
;on the other hand,	-er than
less than	on the contrary
,but	the ____ -est
different	the most
different from	

Write a sentence of contrast for each of the following pairs of words.

EXAMPLE: feather / rock
A feather weighs less than a rock. _____

1. Alaska / Florida

_____

2. gold / silver

_____

3. airplane / train

_____

4. houses / apartments

_____

5. classical music / rock 'n roll

_____

6. Volkswagen / Rolls Royce

_____

7. ice cream / rice

_____

Contrasts

ACTIVITY 1

Read the following paragraph.

When Michael was vacationing in Farmington last month, he ate lunch at the City Avenue Café and dinner at the famous French restaurant, Chez Robert. His lunch was the worst meal he had ever eaten, but fortunately, his dinner was the best meal he had ever eaten. The Café was dirty and noisy; however, Chez Robert was clean and quiet. The waitresses at the Café were rude and the lights were so bright that they bothered his eyes. On the other hand, the waitresses at Chez Robert were polite and attentive, and the only light in the dining room came from candles. Michael will always remember his delicious dinner at Chez Robert, but he can't wait to forget his terrible lunch at the City Avenue Café.

A. Underline the expressions of contrast.

B. Make a list of the differences between the two restaurants:

_____   _____

_____   _____

_____   _____

_____   _____

C. Fill in the blanks in the following sentences:

1. The Café was _____ than Chez Robert.

2. Chez Robert was _____ than _____.

3. The waitresses were _____ at _____ than at _____.

4. The lights were _____ at _____ than at _____.

5. The food at _____ was _____ than at _____.

ACTIVITY 2

Read these advertisements from the classified section of the newspaper.

APTS. RENT

Fairfax Apartments-large 2 bedroom apt. Near campus. Air conditioned. Furnished. No pets. All utilities included. Available Sept. 1. $400/month.

CAMPUS APTS-1 bedroom apt. available immediately in large modern building. Near campus. Unfurnished. Pets allowed. Only $245/month plus utilities.

Write five sentences of contrast about the two apartments.

1. _____

2. _____

3. _____

4. _____

5. _____

ACTIVITY 3

Study the following chart. It gives information about three computer companies.

	Gross Income	Net Income	Year Founded	Number of Employees when Started	Number of Employees Now	Number of Offices
CITY INFORMATION SERVICES	$2,500,000	$150,000	1982	5	22	1
NATIONAL COMPUTER CORPORATION	$6,000,000	$900,000	1984	20	50	3
INTERNATIONAL DATA BASE SYSTEMS	$5,000,000	$1,000,000	1987	2	45	5

Write five sentences of contrast about the three companies.

1. _____

2. _____

3. _____

4. _____

5. _____

Writing a Paragraph of Contrast

ACTIVITY 1

You and a friend are planning a trip to Hawaii. You found these advertisements in the newspaper.

Before Writing

A. Make a list of differences between the two plans.

_____   _____
_____   _____
_____   _____
_____   _____
_____   _____

Writing

B. Write a letter to your friend contrasting the two plans and suggesting the one you think would be better for you.

ACTIVITY 2

You received the following three résumés from people applying for a job in your English program.

Deborah Fines
42 St. James Place
Philadelphia, PA 19106

Position Desired:	English Instructor	
Personal:	Age 28, single, fluent in French	
Education:	1988–92	BA English, University of Michigan
	1991–93	MA English, University of Michigan
	1993–95	PhD Linguistics, University of Pennsylvania
Employment Experience:	1988–93	Waitress
	1993–94	Swimming Teacher
	1994–present	Teaching Assistant, Linguistics Department, University of Pennsylvania
Publication:	"English Verb Tenses," *American Linguistics Journal*	

Lynn Whitnall
242 West 21 Street
New York, New York 19125

Position Desired:

English Instructor

Personal:

Age 35, married, fluent in Spanish, French, Italian

Education:

1985–89	BA Spanish, New York University

Employment Experience:

1990–94	High school Spanish teacher
1994–present	Peace Corps volunteer in Colombia

Seyma Kara
4247 Locust Street
Philadelphia, PA 19140

Position Desired:	English Instructor	
Personal:	Age 27, single, fluent in Turkish	
Education:	1972–76	BA English, University of Michigan
	1976–78	MS TESOL, University of Michigan
Employment Experience:	1984–94	ESL Instructor, English Language Institute, Ann Arbor, Michigan
	1994–present	English Teacher, Marmara University, Istanbul, Turkey

Before Writing

A. Write five sentences of contrast based on the information in the résumés on page 81.

1. _____

2. _____

3. _____

4. _____

5. _____

Who do you think would make the best English instructor?

_____

Writing

B. Write a paragraph supporting your opinion.

ACTIVITY 3

Choose one of the following topics to write about.

- two cities you have visited
- two vacations you have taken
- two jobs you have had
- two athletic teams you like
- two musical instruments you are familiar with

Before Writing

A. Before you begin the first draft of your paragraph, make a list of differences between the two things you are contrasting.

_____

_____

_____

_____

_____

_____

Writing

B. Use the list as your guide to write a paragraph of contrast.

Science Experiment

Scientific experiments are often done to show comparisons and contrasts.

The following experiment shows that copper is a better conductor of heat than wood. You will need to assemble: two strips of paper, a copper rod, a wooden rod, and a candle. First of all, wrap a strip of paper around the copper rod. After that hold the rod above a burning candle for two seconds. Then, examine the paper. You will notice that it did not burn. Now repeat the same procedure with the wooden rod. Notice that this time the paper scorches. This simple experiment proves that copper conducts heat better than wood.

Ready to Write

1. What is being contrasted in this experiment?

_____

2. Write the first draft of a lab report based on this experiment on a separate piece of paper.

Revising
3. Revise your lab report and write your final draft in the space below.

Purpose: _____

Materials: _____

Procedure: _____

Results:

Gathering Data for Comparisons and Contrasts

If you have traveled to or met people from other countries, you know that there are both similarities and differences between cultures. In this activity you are going to write a paragraph focusing on the differences between one aspect of your culture and that same aspect in another culture.

1. Choose one of the following topics for your paragraph:

- eating habits
- social customs
- climate
- education
- tourism

Before Writing
2. • Make a list of questions on your topic that you can ask someone from another country.
   • Make a list of the differences on your topic between your country and your partner's country.

Writing
3. Write a paragraph of contrast using your list as a guide.

Revising
4. Revise and then rewrite your paragraph.

5. Read your paragraph aloud to the class.

You Be the Editor

The following paragraph has nine mistakes. Find the mistakes and correct them. Then, copy the corrected paragraph on a separate piece of paper.

Francisco received a scholarship to study English in the United States. He had a difficulty time deciding whether he should attend the English Program at Miami Community College in Miami, Florida or Rocky Mountain College in Denver, Colorado. It would be a lot cheapest for him to go to the community college, but he realize that his living expenses would be a lot more high in the city. Both schools has an excellent reputation, but Rocky Mountain is a much smaller school with a best student/teacher ratio. If he goes to the community college, he will not be as far away from home and he could go home more oftener. He also thought about how he would spend his free time. He might be happier, comfortabler, and more relaxed in the mountains. Finally, decided to attend Miami Community because the temperature is warmer in Florida and he is used to warm weather and water sports.

Ready to Write

On Your Own

Write a paragraph about participation in sports. Use the bar graph below to make comparisons and contrasts between the participation of males and females in the ten most popular sports activities.

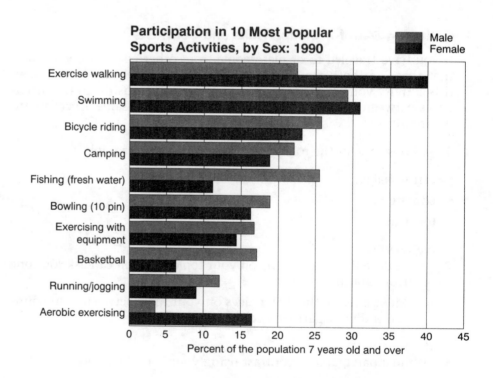

Participation in 10 Most Popular Sports Activities, by Sex: 1990

Male
Female

Exercise walking
Swimming
Bicycle riding
Camping
Fishing (fresh water)
Bowling (10 pin)
Exercising with equipment
Basketball
Running/jogging
Aerobic exercising

0   5   10   15   20   25   30   35   40   45
Percent of the population 7 years old and over

Analyzing a Situation

Analyzing involves examining the parts of a situation, idea, or problem and looking for a relationship among them. Look at these two pictures. Is there a relationship between what happened in picture A and what happened in picture B?

A

B

We can analyze these pictures by asking: Why is the man happy? When you analyze a situation by asking *why*, you will often use a cause–effect relationship.

Study the following sets of pictures. One picture in each group shows a cause. The other one shows an effect. State the cause and effect for each group. Follow the example.

EXAMPLE: Cause: ___*The man found $100.*___   Effect: ___*He was very happy.*___

1.   Cause: _____

    Effect: _____

2. Cause: _____

   Effect: _____

3. Cause: _____

   Effect: _____

4. Cause: _____

   Effect: _____

The Language of Cause and Effect

The following vocabulary and useful expressions will help you analyze cause–effect relationships.

because	;thus	since
,so	because of	the cause of
;therefore,	;consequently,	as a result,

Look at this cartoon. Study the patterns of cause and effect sentences.

By Schulz

1. Snoopy is angry because there are no ice cubes in his water.
2. There are no ice cubes in Snoopy's water; therefore, he is angry.
3. There are no ice cubes in Snoopy's water, so he is angry.
4. Since there are no ice cubes in Snoopy's water, he is angry.

Writing Sentences of Cause and Effect

ACTIVITY 1

Write a sentence of cause and effect for each of the sets of pictures on pages 85 and 86.

EXAMPLE: The man was happy because he found $100.

1. _____

2. _____

3. _____

4. _____

ACTIVITY 2

A. Column *A* below is a list of effects and column *B* is a list of causes. Match the causes and effects. The first one is done for you.

A

I'm going skiing

we moved to the country

we bought a new car

they took an airplane

she took a bus

I have to go by car

I usually walk to work

he rides his bike to work

B

it was faster

he has trouble finding a parking space

the city was too crowded

it snowed five inches last night

I need the exercise

the old one used too much gas

it was cheaper

the train doesn't go there

B. Combine the causes and effects to make new sentences. Use *so, because,* or *therefore.*

EXAMPLE: *He has trouble finding a parking space, so he rides his bike to work.*

Ready to Write

Writing a Paragraph to Analyze a Situation

CLASS ACTIVITY

In this activity you will analyze pollution by discussing some of its causes.

With your classmates and teacher, work through the following steps:

1. Your teacher will put a topic sentence on the chalkboard such as: There are several causes of pollution.

Before Writing

2. What causes can you and your classmates think of? As you think of causes, your teacher will write them in list form on the chalkboard. (Remember, these are just ideas, so they don't have to be in sentence form or correct order.) Copy the list from the chalkboard here.

_____

_____

_____

_____

3. After you have a complete list of causes, discuss them. Decide which should be included in the paragraph. Cross out the ones that are not relevant.

Writing

4. Write a paragraph about the causes of pollution, using your list as a guide. Begin with what you feel is the most important cause. Your teacher will write a paragraph on the chalkboard.

INDIVIDUAL ACTIVITY

In this activity you will analyze an important decision that you have made in your life.

1. Choose an important decision which you have made in your life such as:

- getting married
- coming to an English-speaking country
- picking a school
- choosing a career
- buying a house

Before Writing
2. Analyze either the reasons that led you to make the decision or the effects this decision had on your life. Make a list of the ideas you will want to include in your paragraph.

_____

_____

_____

_____

Writing
3. Write a first draft of your paragraph, using your list as a guide.

Revising
4. Revise and rewrite your paragraph.

SMALL GROUP ACTIVITIES

ACTIVITY 1

Often you analyze a situation or an idea by examining its advantages and/or its disadvantages. In this activity, you will analyze the advantages of living in the city.

Before Writing
A. With three or four of your classmates, analyze the advantages of living in a city. Discuss and make a list of the advantages you think of.

Advantages of living in a big city

_____

_____

_____

_____

Writing
B. Write a paragraph based on your list. Organize your ideas according to the order of their importance. Save the biggest advantage for the last.

C. Follow the same procedure with the disadvantages of living in the city.

ACTIVITY 2

You are a business administration student. You have been asked to analyze the following case history:

CASE HISTORY #6

anal in Venice. It is
ly this kind of
ograph. But an
work of art is not
me of the buildings
look bigger than
ie look smaller. The
he one in the
ant to copy
wanted to paint

On September 5, Michael Williams opened a small compact disc shop in the basement of the Fairfax Apartment Building. The apartment building is located on a small side street just outside of town. It is three miles away from a large shopping center that has two discount compact disc stores.

Mr. Williams spent $10,000 buying CDs for his shop. Most of the CDs were rock 'n 'roll. He sold each CD for $8.00. He hired three people to work as salespersons and paid them $5.50 an hour. The shop was open Monday–Friday from 1–5 P.M. Mr. Williams would not accept checks or credit cards.

On December 19, Mr. Williams closed his shop. He put a sign on the door that said "Out of Business."

A. Discuss this case in your group. Why do you think the business failed? Make a list of the causes.

_____

_____

_____

_____

_____

_____

_____

_____

_____

_____

_____

Residents of the Fairfax by Age Groups

Age of Residents	Number of Residents
0–10 years	14
10–20	3
20–30	20
30–40	25
40–50	45
50–60	57
60 +	43

B. Now study this table:

1. How can you describe the people who live in the Fairfax? What generalization can you make about the people?

_____

2. Can you use the information on this table to think of another cause of the failure of this business?

_____

Add it to your original list of causes.

C. Now study this table:

Number of People Who Walk Past the Store

	MON	TUES	WED	THURS	FRI	SAT	SUN
Number of people passing in the morning 8AM–12PM	30	35	28	29	31	32	20
In the afternoon 12–6PM	10	12	16	15	20	70	65
In the evening 6PM–12AM	40	47	53	42	60	65	40

Write three statements based on this table.

1. _____

2. _____

3. _____

Can you use the information on this table to think of another cause of the failure?

_____

Add it to your list of causes.

Writing
D. Write a first draft of a paragraph discussing the causes of the failure of Mr. Williams's compact disc shop.

Revising
E. Revise and rewrite your group's paragraph.

ACTIVITY 3

Plants and animals affect each other in many ways. Look at the diagram below. It shows how plants and animals depend on each other in a farm pond. You have been asked to write a short explanation of this diagram for a children's science magazine.

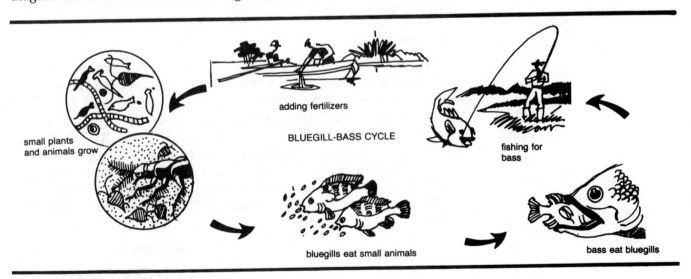

adding fertilizers

BLUEGILL-BASS CYCLE

small plants and animals grow

fishing for bass

bluegills eat small animals

bass eat bluegills

Write a paragraph on a separate sheet of paper about the ecological relationships that are shown in the diagram.

Just For Fun

Match the questions in column *A* with the answers in column *B*.

A	**B**
1. Why did the man cross the street?	_____ His head is so far from his body.
2. Why did the man throw the clock out the window?	_____ They live in schools.
3. Why does the giraffe have such a long neck?	_____ He wanted to see time fly.
4. Why did the man tiptoe past the medicine cabinet?	_____ He wanted to get to the other side.
5. Why are fish smarter than insects?	_____ He didn't want to wake up the sleeping pills.
6. Why is a library the tallest building?	_____ It has the largest number of stories.

You Be the Editor

Read the following letter, which complains about an inferior product. It contains seven mistakes. Correct the mistakes and rewrite the corrected letter on a separate sheet of paper.

1123 Gardner Street
Swansea, Massachusetts 02777
March 2, 1998

Youth Fair Cosmetics Company
234 Philip Place
New York, New York

Dear Sir,

I have been using youth fair products for many years and I have always been very pleased with them. However, last week I bought a bottle of your newest perfume, Rose Petal, and had dreadful results. First, it stained my blouse. It also cause my skin to itch and burn. Worst of all, I couldn't stop sneezing after used it. I feel that this product does not meet your standards of high quality and I would appreciate receiving a refund. I look forward to hearing from you on this matter in the near future.

sincerely

Charlotte Sherden

Charlotte Sherden

On Your Own

1. Analyze a recent economic or political situation in your country by examining either its causes or effects.

2. Analyze the advantages or disadvantages of living in a small town.

3. Analyze the effects of white sugar on the human body, using the following list of facts as a guide.

- robs the body of vitamin B
- causes tooth decay
- interferes with calcium metabolism
- contributes to hardening of arteries

Making Predictions

CHAPTER 13

"What do you think happens next?"

The Language of Prediction

1. Read this story.

It is a cold, rainy night. Jane Richardson leaves Raka's Restaurant alone. She walks down Main Street and turns onto the poorly lit street where her car is parked. She looks quickly to the left and to the right. She sees something move in the shadows. She jumps.

What do you think happens next?

2. As you can see, the story has not been finished. In groups of three or four, discuss what you think will happen next. How do you think the story will end? Choose one person in the group to write down some of your ideas. Compare your group's ending with those of the other groups.

In this activity you made a guess about the future. This is called *prediction*.

Sometimes you will need to use *if* sentences to make a prediction. Look at the following advertisements. Both of them make predictions. They tell what will happen if you use a certain product.

EXAMPLES:
a. If you use Silky Cream, your hands will be soft and smooth.
b. If you use Light and Bright Toothpaste, you will have fewer cavities.

1. _____

2. _____

3. Notice the structure and the verb tenses in *if* sentences. Write advertisements for the following products using sentences with *if*. Make a prediction about what will happen if you use these products.

3. _____   4. _____

5. _____   6. _____

Writing Paragraphs of Prediction

INDIVIDUAL ACTIVITY

Write a paragraph on a separate sheet of paper predicting what one of the following will be like fifty years from now.

a. Transportation   c. Housing   e. Medicine
b. Clothing   d. Food   f. Communication

SMALL-GROUP ACTIVITY

Read the following paragraphs.

Westport is a small town in the Midwest. It has a population of 2,500. It is a safe, quiet, and clean place to live. Most of the people have lived there all their lives and know each other very well. The town has not changed very much in the past one hundred years.

Last month, Stanley Manufacturing decided to open a large factory in Westport. This will bring many new people to the community. Some people are worried about the negative effects the new factory will have on the town. Other people are excited about the positive effects the new factory will have on Westport.

Before Writing

In small groups make predictions about the impact the new factory will have on Westport. Make a list of all the possible effects you can think of.

Positive	Negative
more jobs	*pollution*

Writing

a. You are a conservative resident who doesn't want to see change. Write a paragraph predicting the negative effects the factory will have on the town.

b. You are a progressive businessman. Write a paragraph predicting the positive effects the new factory will have on the town.

Using Quotations to Support a Prediction

ACTIVITY 1

Read the following paragraph.

Many weather forecasters are predicting that this winter will be colder than usual in the United States. There are many reasons why meteorologists believe this is going to be a long, hard winter. First of all, August was a very cool month. As a result, many parts of Canada never warmed up and the ground is already cold. Secondly, recent studies show that the sun has been putting out less energy for the past two years. Climatologists know that in the past, a decline in solar energy has meant a change to colder weather. Finally, Mexico's El Chicon volcano created a cloud of dust and acid. This is shielding the earth from sunlight.

Each of the following quotations can be used to support the weather forecasters' predictions. Rewrite the paragraph, putting these quotes where they are appropriate.

- "This is troubling because even a small reduction of solar energy can affect agriculture worldwide." Stephen Schneider.

- "There are twenty-two volcanoes around the globe sending tons of sulphur dioxide into the atmosphere. It just sits there and reflects sunlight." Reid Bryson

ACTIVITY 2

Write a caption for this cartoon.

_____

How would your grandparents react to this cartoon? What kind of caption do you think they might write?

_____

You Be the Editor

Read the following paragraph about investing money. There are seven errors. Correct the errors and rewrite the paragraph in its corrected form.

When John St. Marker sold his telemarketing business, he made a great deal of money. He received a lot of advice about how to invest it. His brother said to him, "now is a good time to invest in Real Estate because the market is very active and you might double your investment." A stockbroker told him, "You should diversify. If you invest in both stocks and bonds, you will do very good. We are all predicting that the market will go more higher this year, and the bond market is usually pretty stable." John decided to take the advices of both men. He invested 30 percent of his money in real estate, 30 percent in stocks, and 30 percent in bonds. In this way, he hopes to protect his families future.

On Your Own

1. How do you think advances in technology will affect family life in the future? Discuss your ideas in paragraph form.

2. Look at the graph about Springfield Academy on page 32. What predictions can you make about the future enrollment of the school?

Writing Summaries

> "A summary gives only main ideas. It does not include details."

The Language of Summaries

Summaries require a special kind of writing. A good summary gives only main ideas. It does not include details. Before you begin to write, you should think about *who, when, where, why, what,* and *how.*

ACTIVITY 1

Follow these steps:

A. Read the following article very carefully.

George Washington Carver was born in 1864 in Diamond Grove, Missouri. He and his family were slaves. As a child, he was very interested in plants. He became known as the plant doctor because he knew so much about them and he was so good at making them grow. He was also a very good student and always interested in learning. He worked his way through Iowa State College. In 1894, he graduated with a degree in agriculture. He was the first African-American graduate of the school, and he later became the first African-American faculty member there. Carver won many awards and medals for his work in agricultural chemistry. His major goal in life was to help African-Americans in the South. He showed them how to improve the soil by rotating cotton crops with peanut and sweet potato crops. He knew that this would make the soil better and also provide new sources of income. He then experimented and discovered over three hundred new uses for the peanut and the sweet potato such as medicines, plastics, flour, glue, fertilizer, and cereal.

Underline the important ideas.

Before Writing
B. Make a list of the important facts in the article. Be sure to include *what, where, when, who,* and *why* on your list.

Ready to Write

_____

_____

_____

_____

_____

Study your list. Make sure you have included only the main ideas. Cross out any items on your list that are details.

C. Write the ideas on the list in full sentences. Try to combine some of the ideas with *and, but, or, however, because,* and so on.

• Make sure your list is in a logical sequence.

Writing
D. Write a short, one-paragraph summary of the article.
Revising
E. Compare your summary with some of your classmates' summaries. Have you included too much information? Are your sentences in a logical sequence?

ACTIVITY 2

Read this short article.

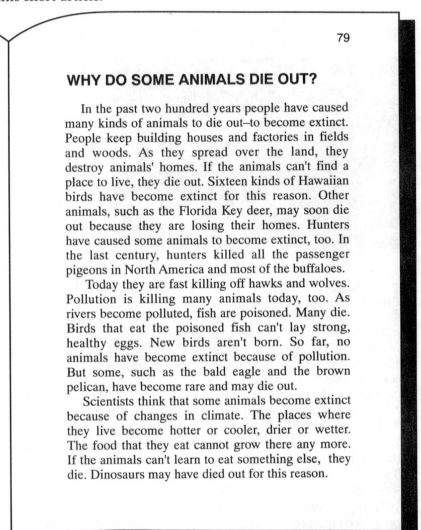

79

WHY DO SOME ANIMALS DIE OUT?

In the past two hundred years people have caused many kinds of animals to die out–to become extinct. People keep building houses and factories in fields and woods. As they spread over the land, they destroy animals' homes. If the animals can't find a place to live, they die out. Sixteen kinds of Hawaiian birds have become extinct for this reason. Other animals, such as the Florida Key deer, may soon die out because they are losing their homes. Hunters have caused some animals to become extinct, too. In the last century, hunters killed all the passenger pigeons in North America and most of the buffaloes.

Today they are fast killing off hawks and wolves. Pollution is killing many animals today, too. As rivers become polluted, fish are poisoned. Many die. Birds that eat the poisoned fish can't lay strong, healthy eggs. New birds aren't born. So far, no animals have become extinct because of pollution. But some, such as the bald eagle and the brown pelican, have become rare and may die out.

Scientists think that some animals become extinct because of changes in climate. The places where they live become hotter or cooler, drier or wetter. The food that they eat cannot grow there any more. If the animals can't learn to eat something else, they die. Dinosaurs may have died out for this reason.

A. Write a one-paragraph summary of the article. The following questions should help you.
1. *What* is the article about? What is happening to many animals?
2. *Why* is it happening?
3. *Where* is it happening?
4. *Who* is responsible?
5. *What* is responsible?
Revising
B. 1. Make sure that you have answered all of the questions above.
2. Look at the revising checklist on page 28.
3. Exchange papers with a partner and edit each other's papers. Did you both include the same information? If not, what were the differences?

4. Rewrite your paragraph.

ACTIVITY 3

Read the following article about the Morgan Motor Company.

If you visit the *Morgan Motor Company* factory in Malvern, England, you will feel as though you have gone back in time to the 1920s or 1930s. You will see telephones, a photocopying machine, and other modern equipment, but you will soon realize that the cars are still made the old-fashioned way. Each *Morgan*, even today, is built by hand. For this reason, no two *Morgans* are ever exactly the same. In addition, the factory can make only about ten cars per week. The result is that there is a five-to-seven-year waiting list for a new *Morgan*, and the older, used ones are very much in demand.

If you are thinking about buying a *Morgan*, there are some things that you should know about yourself and about *Morgans*. If you like an easy ride, power steering and brakes, and a car radio, you probably do not want a *Morgan*.

If, however, you like the feel of the wind in your hair, quick response steering, and a bumpy ride during which you feel every stick and pothole in the road, and if you want the motoring thrill of a lifetime, then buy yourself a *Morgan* and enjoy it.

If a friend of yours were thinking of buying a sports car, how would you summarize this article in a letter to him or her?

You Be the Editor

Read the article at left about electronic mail. There are ten mistakes. Correct the mistakes and then copy the article over.

Experts say that the use of electronic mail (also known as "e-mail") is growing dramatically. According to the Yankee Group, a Boston market-research company, the number of E-mail users in U.S. raised by 60 percents from 5.9 millions to 9.4 millions between 1992 and 1993, and it increased other 60 percent in 1993. Billions of messages are transmitted annual in North America, but accurate figures for worldwide transmission are not available. E-mail is become more and more valuable because it makes communication so much easyier.

On Your Own

Find an article in a book, magazine, or newspaper. Read it carefully and write a one-paragraph summary of it. Bring the article and your summary to class.

Answering Essay Test Questions

Teachers and professors often give essay tests. An essay test requires you to write a complete answer in paragraph form.

Important things to remember when you take an essay test are:

1. Read the entire question carefully.
2. Make sure you understand exactly what information you are being asked to write about (reasons, definitions, etc.).
3. Plan your answer.
4. Budget your time.

ACTIVITY 1

You will find that the easiest way to begin your essay is to change the question to a statement and use this statement as your topic sentence.

EXAMPLE: Question: Discuss why Americans move so often.
Topic sentence: There are many reasons why Americans move often.

Change the following essay questions into topic sentences.

1. Question: Discuss why many women are waiting until after they are thirty years old to have babies.

Topic Sentence: _____.

2. Question: Discuss the effects of radiation on the human body.

Topic Sentence: _____.

3. Question: Discuss the reasons ice hockey is a dangerous sport.

Topic Sentence: _____.

4. Question: Discuss the importance of John F. Kennedy in American history.

Topic Sentence: _____.

5. Question: Discuss the reasons why so many tourists visit South America.

Topic Sentence: _____.

6. Question: Explain the reasons for the popularity of video games.

Topic Sentence: _____.

7. Question: Discuss the advantages and disadvantages of solar energy.

Topic Sentence: _____.

8. Question: Describe the four kinds of clouds.

Topic Sentence: _____.

9. Question: Describe the four stages involved in cell division.

Topic Sentence: _____.

10. Question: Discuss three important causes of inflation.

Topic Sentence: _____.

ACTIVITY 2

Look at the following essay question and answer.

Question: Discuss the three stages of sending a spacecraft into orbit.

Answer:

There are three stages involved in sending a spacecraft into orbit. First, the Stage One Rocket is used for the blastoff, but it is only used for two and a half minutes. When the spacecraft reaches a speed of 6,000 miles per hour and an altitude of forty miles, this rocket drops off into the sea. Then, the Stage Two Rocket is used, but only for about six minutes, because it drops off when the spacecraft reaches a speed of 14,000 miles per hour and an altitude of 110 miles. Finally, during the third stage, the spacecraft goes into orbit. The Stage Three Rocket is used for two minutes, or until the spacecraft reaches a speed of 17,500 miles per hour and an altitude of 120 miles.

Notice that the topic sentence restates the question.

A. Circle the transition words that helped you understand the answer.

B. Underline the specific information—the details, such as numbers and times.

Taking an Essay Test

Choose one of the essay test topics below and write your answer.

1. Discuss the history of computers from 1950 to the present. Base your answer on the following information.

First Generation of Computers	Second Generation of Computers	Third Generation of Computers
–1950–1960	–1960–1965	–1965–present
–electronic tube used as basis of technology	–transistor used as basis of technology	–printed circuit board used as basis of technology
–slow compared to today	–smaller	–smaller
–small data memory bank	–faster	–faster
	–more reliable	–more reliable
	–increased use for business purposes	–less expensive
		–growth in business use
		–growth in use of personal computers

2. Read the following two paragraphs. The first paragraph describes the human eye. The second paragraph describes a camera.

The human eye has an iris that gets bigger or smaller to let in the right amount of light. It also has a lens that focuses the light into a clear picture. In the eye, light forms a picture on the retina. The nerve cells in the retina send a picture message to the brain. The picture the brain receives is upside down. The brain then interprets the message so that what you see is right side up.

The camera has a diaphragm that gets bigger or smaller to let in the right amount of light. It also has a lens that focuses the light into a clear picture. In a camera, light forms a picture on film. The picture is upside down on the film.

Question: There are many similarities between the eye and the camera. Write one paragraph on a separate sheet of paper comparing the eye and the camera.

ANSWER KEY

Chapter 4, page 29.
You Be the Editor

Erik enjoy◯ many types of sports. He (is liking) team sport◯ such as basketball, soccer, and baseball. He also plays traditional(s), individual sports like racquetball and golf◯ (h)is favorite sports involve danger as well as excit(ing.)He loves parasailing, extreme skiing, and skydiving.

Chapter 5, page 37.
You Be the Editor

(t)hroughout history, man has found it nessary to do mathematical computations and keep accounts. (i)n early times, he used groups of sticks or stones to help make calcualtions. (t)hen the abacus was developed in (C)hina. (t)hese simple methods represent the beginnings of data processing. (a)s man's computational needs became more complicated, he developed more advanced technologies. (o)ne example is the first simple adding machine that (m)r. (C)harles (b)abbage designed in 1830. (i)n the middle of the twentieth century, researchers at the (u)niversity of (p)ennsylvania built the first electronic computer. (t)oday of course we have the computer to perform all kinds of advanced mathematical computations.

Chapter 6, page 44.
You Be the Editor

Dear Editor:

In my opinion, it is important for women with small children(s) to work outside of the home. First of all,◯ is (to) difficult to be with little kids all day. Women(s) need(s) a break from th(ere) kids. Also, a woman who has a career can offer her children more(s), because it is the quality of time that mothers spend with their children that (are) important.

Sincerely,
Lisa Harris

Chapter 7, page 50.

You Be the Editor

It is not difficult to remove the shell from a lobster if you follow these step○. First, you should (to) put the lobster on it○s back and remove the two large claws and tail section. After that, (Y)ou must also twist off the flippers at ○ end of ○ tail section. After these are twisted off, use you○ fingers to push the lobster meat out of the tail in one piece. Next, remove the black vein○. (F)rom the tail meat. Finally, before you sit down to enjoy your meal, break open the claws with a nutcracker and remove the meat.

Chapter 8, page 56.

You Be the Editor

```
                           MEMO


     TO:      All Employees
     FROM:    David Stanson, President
     DATE:    3/13/98
     RE:      Punctuality
```

①t has come (recently) to my attention that we are becoming increasingly lax about beginning our work day (in) 9 A.M. I understand that many of you are always on time and I thank you for your reliability○ I also realize that sometimes lateness cannot be avoided. I feel, however, that habitual (late) has become a serious problem and that I must mention it before it gets (worser). It is my opinion that we are a team and that we must all work together to build ○ strongest company we can. Inattention to punctuality creates resentment among coworkers. I (will) appreciate it if you pay(ing) more attention to this important detail in the future.

Chapter 9, page 62.

You Be the Editor

The police (is) looking for a tall, teenage boy with blue(s) eyes in connection with a robbery yesterday at Dayton's Jewelry Store. According to an eye witness, the robber(y) is approximately six (foots) two inches tall, very thin, and his skin is a very light color. He has dark, straight hair(s). He has (a) broad shoulders and a dimple in his chin. His most distinguishing mark is a mole (behind) his right eye. He was last seen wearing a brown suede jacket and (a) brown pant ○. If you see anyone fitting this description, contact the police department immediately.

Chapter 10, page 67.

You Be the Editor

Do Diets Work?

Doctors and dieters agree that ○ is possible to lose weight by dieting. The difficult(y) part, they report, is keeping the weight (of) after you (to) lose it.

Research indicates that many people successfully lose weight at some point in life, but most people gain the weight back within three years. Ian Fenn is a doctor who specializes in weight problems. He says that there (is) many sorts of diets, and medical science is working to figure out how to control body weight. "It is also a matter"(,) he says, "of getting people to change their lifestyles. Each person need(s) to find the right combination of diet and exercise for (them)."

Chapter 11, page 84.

You Be the Editor

Francisco received a scholarship to study English in the United States. He had a difficult(y) time deciding whether he should attend the English program at Miami Community College in Miami, Florida or Rocky Mountain College in Denver, Colorado. It would be a lot cheap(est) for him to go to the community college, but he realize○ that his living expenses would be a lot (more high) in the city. Both schools ha(s) an excellent reputation, but Rocky Mountain is a much smaller school with a (best) student/teacher ratio. If he goes to the community college, he will not be as far away from home and he could go home more often(er). He also thought about how he would spend his free time. He might be happier, comfortabl(er) and more relaxed in the mountains. Finally, ○decided to attend Miami Community because the temperature is warmer in Florida and he is used to warm weather and water sports.

Chapter 12, page 92.
You Be the Editor

1123 Gardner Street
Swansea, Massachusetts 02777
March 2, 1998

Youth Fair Cosmetics Company
234 Philip Place
New York, New York

Dear Sir(,)

I have been using (Y)outh (F)air products for many years and I have always been very pleased with them. However, last week I bought a bottle of your newest perfume, Rose Petal, and had dreadful results. First, it stained my blouse. It also cause(d) my skin to itch and burn. Worst of all, I couldn't stop sneezing after (I) used it. I feel that this product does not meet your standards of high quality and I would appreciate receiving a refund. I look forward to hearing from you on this matter in the near future.

(S)incerely(,)

Charlotte Sherden

Charlotte Sherden

Chapter 13, page 97.
You Be the Editor

When John St. Marker sold his telemarketing business, he made a great deal of money. He received a lot of advice about how to invest it. His brother said to him, ("n)ow is a good time to invest in (R)eal (E)state because the market is very active and you might double your investment." A stockbroker told him, "You should diversify. If you invest in both stocks and bonds, you will do very (good). We are all predicting that the market will go (more) higher this year, and the bond market is usually pretty stable." John decided to take the advice(s) of both men. He invested 30 percent of his money in real estate, 30 percent in stocks, and 30 percent in bonds. In this way, he hopes to protect his famil(ies) future.

You Be the Editor

Experts say that the use of electronic mail (also known as "e-mail") is growing dramatically. According to the Yankee Group, a Boston market-research company, the number of ~E-mail~ users in ◯ U.S. ⟨raised⟩ by 60 percent⟨s⟩ from 5.9 million⟨s⟩ to 9.4 million⟨s⟩ between 1992 and 1993, and it increased ⟨other⟩ 60 percent in 1993. Billions of messages are transmitted ⟨annual⟩ in North America, but accurate figures for worldwide transmission are not available. E-mail is becom⟨e⟩ more and more valuable because it makes communication so much ⟨easyier⟩.

Credits

1. Page 16. Reproduced from the Ladybird book *Talkabout Holidays* with the permission of the publishers, Ladybird Books Limited. Loughborough, England.
2. Page 31. News article by Peter M. Jones, reproduced with permission of *Senior Scholastic Magazine;* pie charts from "The Economic Development of Mexico," by P. G. Casanova. Copyright 1980 by Scientific American, Inc. All rights reserved.
3. Page 32. Reprinted courtesy of *The Boston Globe.*
4. Page 34. Reprinted with permission from *Open Doors: 1991–92,* The Institute of International Education.
5. Page 35. Reprinted with permission from *The Complete Book of Running,* by James F. Fixx, © 1977 by Random House, Inc.
6. Page 58. Photo by Linda Borish.
7. Page 63. Adapted by permission of *News for You,* published by New Readers Press, publishing division of Laubach Literacy International, Box 131, Syracuse, New York 13210, July 7, 1982.
8. Page 84. Chart prepared by U.S. Bureau of the Census for the *Statistical Abstract of the United States, 1992,* p. 230.
9. Page 91. From the *Golden Stamp Book of Earth and Ecology* by George S. Fichter, © 1972 Western Publishing Company, Inc. Used by permission.
10. Page 96. Reprinted by permission of Joseph Farris.
11. Page 100. Adapted from *The Illustrated Morgan Buyer's Guide,* by Ken Hill, Motorbooks International Publishers & Wholesalers, Osceola, Wisconsin 54020.
12. PEANUTS reprinted by permission of UFS, Inc.